BEETH[VEN'S]
PIANO PLAYING

With an Essay on the Execution of the Trill

FRANZ KULLAK

Edited with New Examples,
and an Introduction by
ANTON KUERTI

Dover Publications, Inc.
Mineola, New York

Bibliographical Note

This Dover edition, first published in 2013, is an unabridged republication of the work originally published by G. Schirmer, New York, in 1901. Anton Kuerti has prepared a new Introduction and musical examples specially for this Dover edition.

Library of Congress Cataloging-in-Publication Data

Kullak, Franz, 1844–1913, author.
  Beethoven's piano playing : with an essay on the execution of the trill / Franz Kullak; edited with new examples and an introduction by Anton Kuerti.
     p. cm.
  ISBN-13: 978-0-486-49968-0
  ISBN-10: 0-486-49968-5
  1. Beethoven, Ludwig van, 1770–1827. 2. Piano—Instruction and study.
I. Kuerti, Anton, editor. II. Title.

MT220.K99 2013
786.2092—dc23

                                                                    2013012733

Manufactured in the United States by Courier Corporation
49968501   2013
www.doverpublications.com

INTRODUCTION TO THE DOVER EDITION

Franz Kullak (1844–1913) is a shining example of a conscientious nineteenth-century music editor of great integrity. His editions of Beethoven's Piano Concerti were published in 1901 by G. Schirmer in New York. While the omnipresent yellow Schirmer editions are generally not admired by serious musicians, Kullak's are superb. Even the new complete Beethoven edition, created by scholars of the Beethoven-Haus in Bonn and published by G. Henle in Munich, displays only the most minuscule deviations from the Kullak version, and in certain respects is actually less satisfactory (for lack of footnotes explaining some of their choices).

Kullak was determined to reproduce Beethoven's music exactly as the composer wrote it, nothing added nor subtracted (except for copious footnotes where Beethoven's intentions were in doubt). This approach was almost unheard of in the nineteenth century, which was replete with unscrupulous editors who arrogated to themselves the right to "improve" the works of the great masters by changing details of phrasing, dynamics, tempo, expression marks, and yes, even the notes themselves. This attitude can only be characterized as artistic vandalism.

Among the many who tampered irresponsibly with Beethoven's piano works were the well-known musicians Eugen d'Albert, Harold Bauer, Hans von Bülow, Alfredo Casella, Harold Craxton, Leopold Godowsky, Frederic Lamond, Sigmund Lebert, Max Pauer, Hugo Riemann, Artur Schnabel, and Leo Weiner.

It is fitting that Dover Publications should reprint Franz Kullak's essay on Beethoven's piano playing, which originally appeared as an introduction to his edition of the Beethoven Piano Concerti. Kullak researched the information in this essay just as assiduously as he did the sources of his scores. It embraces accounts from a broad range of individuals, including "ear-witnesses" like Beethoven's students Carl Czerny and Ferdinand Ries, his fellow composers Luigi Cherubini and Johann Cramer, his first biographer Anton Schindler, and two biographers of a later generation who were avid collectors of Beethoveniana, Gustav Nottebohm and Alexander Wheelock Thayer.

Introduction to the Dover Edition

A memorable portrait emerges of Beethoven as an extremely energetic and profound performer, with a certain affinity for legato and vivid characterization, but often inaccurate and inconsistent. However, this image does not resolve without considerable contradictions, particularly in the realm of liberties and tempo modifications. Many, including Czerny, stressed that Beethoven played quite strictly in time.

Anton Schindler, on the other hand, wrote several "play by play" descriptions of Beethoven's performances that indicate he was at times prepared to change tempi almost from bar to bar. Here is his description of the master's performance of the first movement of the Sonata in E Major Op. 14, No. 1:

> *"In the 8th bar of the first movement Allegro he retarded the tempo, and extended the 4th right hand note. Thus he conveyed an indescribable earnestness and dignity. In the 10th bar he resumed the original tempo, but the following bars were played diminuendo and a little held back. At the second subject, the tempo became Andante, but irregular, giving the first note of the descending theme a little fermata. In the next phrase he returned to the original tempo, but in the development he broadened the rhythm ... where the second movement arrives at a long chord he made a very lengthy fermata ... in every movement* [referring to a whole group of sonatas] *Beethoven varied the tempo as the mood changed."* [1]

The degree of tempo modifications in this report may be exaggerated, especially as Schindler is known to have been unscrupulous at times (for example, he added content to Beethoven's conversation books after the composer's death). Still, it is my opinion that his descriptions absolutely conform to the spirit of the music, and ring true.

A possible explanation for the widely diverging opinions on the degree of liberty Beethoven allowed himself is that some performers of the day permitted themselves such outrageous excesses that by comparison it seemed Beethoven played very strictly. Czerny, though testifying to Beethoven's steadiness of tempo, on the other hand gave detailed interpretative instructions in his *Complete Theoretical and*

---

1 All translations are by the author.

Introduction to the Dover Edition

Practical Piano Forte School Op. 500, to the effect of "play a little faster here, slow down there, hold this chord a bit longer," etc.

The imaginative performer will not attempt to align his or her inspiration to the cruel, unyielding tick of a metronome. Every piece of music, indeed every movement, is a unique creation. According to their individual character, some, like the finale of Beethoven's Sonata Op. 31, No. 2 (the "Tempest"), require an absolute steadiness of tempo; others, like the Sonata Op. 14, No.1 described above, or the improvisatory second subject of Op. 109, need daring doses of flexibility to fully bring out their extraordinary flavor. The divergent testimony of those close to Beethoven may also be related to exactly which works they heard him play.

The great performer will allow each note to find its most exquisite personal length, without imposing a calculated distortion on the composition. As in every detail of interpretation, the line dividing great artistry from mannered exhibitionism is elusive, hard to find, and easy to violate; while a timid approach to these matters may facilitate a decent performance, it will never result in a towering one. Better to risk offending the listener than to take refuge in unassailable competence.

Kullak devotes quite a few pages to a discussion of metronome marks; he quotes Beethoven as saying: *"No metronome at all! Whoever has the right feeling, needs none; and whoever lacks it, has no use for one..."* On another occasion, Beethoven wrote a metronome mark on a manuscript, followed by *"this applies only to the first bar, for feeling has its own tempo, which cannot be expressed by a number,"* thus giving more credibility to Schindler's description of Beethoven's tempo changes.

Another interesting remark, written in 1824 by Schindler in one of Beethoven's conversation books, is: *"[we] were surprised that you deviated so markedly from the accelerated tempi of former years, and that now you consider everything to be too fast. Master, may your young 'son' say what he feels about this? I would have liked to embrace you at the rehearsal yesterday, when you gave us all the reasons why you now feel your works differently than 15 to 20 years ago. I confess that I was not in agreement with various tempi during that period ... it was clearly noticeable, and observed by many, that you now wanted all the allegros slower ... what a remarkable difference! How much emerged from the inner voices that was previously impossible to hear and often muddled."* Unfortunately, Beethoven's answers were rarely written down, so we will never know his response.

Introduction to the Dover Edition

I choose to ignore the metronome marks when they are in blatant contradiction to the written tempo marking. For example, the Fugue of the "Hammerklavier" Sonata Op. 106, is marked "Allegro risoluto." At the metronome marking of 144 to the quarter note, the result can only be "Allegro isterico." (Luckily, this sonata is the only piano work bearing Beethoven's own metronome marks!)

The largest portion of Kullak's treatise, 58 out of 101 pages, is devoted to the execution of the trill. This is an outstanding and thorough study, quoting every important source. While it is important for musicians to be acquainted with the known historical practices relating to ornaments, a performance will be neither destroyed nor exalted by choosing to start a particular trill from the main note or its upper neighbor.

The key point about ornamentation is that it implies a certain freedom of choice. Even in the music of Bach, whose trills generally start from above, there are numerous spots where this is impossible, as it would create ugly parallel fifths or octaves. See the following example, from Invention No. 15, BWV 786.

To avoid those, the eighteenth-century musician would no doubt have instinctively played such trills before the beat.

An interesting bit of evidence is found in the complete works of Haydn, Hob.XIX:1–32. He wrote several pieces for mechanical organ, and the performance of some of these devices, built in his lifetime, has been deciphered, showing that some ornaments start from above, some don't, some are on the beat, others before the beat.

Practices were changing during Beethoven's lifetime, and there are certainly some trills in his works which should start from above, and some which shouldn't, like the opening of the Violin Sonata Op. 96.

Introduction to the Dover Edition

In this particular trill it would also be best to forego making an after-beat. Most trills in Beethoven can safely be executed either way; generally, starting with the more dissonant note is best. Almost always, the gifted performer's intuition will quickly provide an acceptable choice, though it may differ from that of others.

While Kullak dwells extensively on how to begin trills, he does not say much about how to end them. In this respect Beethoven could appear to be annoyingly arbitrary, often writing in an afterbeat while omitting it in analogous spots, until one realizes that he usually writes it only when an accidental is needed on one of the notes. (See the last movement of the "Hammerklavier" Sonata.) An afterbeat is always permissible, though not always desirable, as in Example 2.

There are many issues about the interpretation of Beethoven's scores that are much more important than how to begin a trill, and I would have preferred to get Kullak's opinions on some of those. In their absence I will venture to add some of my own thoughts.

One of the most important questions relates to the various symbols that determine the length and emphasis of notes. In an 1825 letter, Beethoven writes: *"For heaven's sake impress on Kempel* [his copyist] *to copy everything just as it stands ... when a dot is placed over a note, a stroke* [the short vertical line above or below the notehead]·*is not to take its place, and vice versa. It is not the same thing to write* ⌐ ⌐ ⌐ *as to write* ⌐ ⌐ ⌐ *... I have spent the whole morning today and yesterday afternoon correcting these two pieces, and I am quite hoarse from swearing and stamping."* In any number of other letters he insists that the publishers send him proofs to correct, and castigates them for not copying precisely what he wrote.

However, most older editions did not even bother to distinguish between staccato dots and strokes, either printing them all as dots, or all as strokes. I cannot remember any of my teachers commenting on the meaning of the stroke. In fact, that very term was unfamiliar to me, and to this day I remain unsure what to call that dark, sometimes tear-shaped line. Yet a correct understanding of it is indispensable for playing properly and beautifully.

In German it is called a *strich*, or, depending on how fat it is, a *keil*. But here even the well-organized Germans show considerable confusion because *strich* just means a "line" and can indicate a horizontal tenuto line as well as a vertical stroke.

Introduction to the Dover Edition

Judging solely by its pictorial character, one well might (and many do) assume that a stroke is simply a staccato with a vengeance—which may well be the case for some later composers. Strokes have variously been called wedges, carets, even daggers. Some people even refer to them as "staccatissimo," but this is *way off the mark* as I shall try to prove below.

In resolving such questions I strongly distrust the role of tradition (i.e. hearsay passed down through a chain of teachers.) Over the years, tradition can too easily and promiscuously mingle with and become undistinguishable from one's own instincts and habits; and it is far too convenient to exploit it as a crutch to support opinions for which no other substantiation exists.

I also avoid invoking "authorities," whether of the past or the present, for they often disagree with each other. A 1957 booklet published by Baerenreiter, "Die Bedeutung der Zeichen Keil, Strich und Punkt bei Mozart," has essays on dots and strokes by five musicologists. Some say the stroke is longer than the dot, others say the opposite, one says that they are identical in meaning. Quantz seems to indicate that the stroke is longer, while Leopold Mozart implies it is shorter. This tangle of opinions is disconcerting, and leads us back to the best authority of all: the "inside evidence," drawn entirely from the composer's scores—and there is plenty of it to resolve this question quite unambiguously.

It is unfortunate that in this respect even the finest editions do not serve us well. The Preface to the new Beethoven-Haus Complete Works Edition states that *"As shortening symbols* [Kürzezeichen—an expression which already begs the question] *Beethoven used strokes and dots variably and inconsistently. They are therefore all reproduced as dots in our Complete Works Edition. When on the other hand Beethoven uses strokes as symbols of accentuation (usually recognizable by their being diagonal), then they are reproduced as a 'keil'* [stroke]. *"* But who is to decide when the strokes are meant to indicate shortness, and when they indicate accentuation? While they are indeed often diagonal, every possible variation of angle can be found, and they often change in the course of a passage or at analogous spots. Furthermore, Beethoven writes far more strokes than dots, so it would have been truer to the text to reproduce them all as strokes, rather than dots.

As Beethoven's handwriting requires a cryptographer to decipher even the notes, it is indeed an exceedingly challenging task to make sense of all this in a published edition, for the dot-hood or stroke-hood of a goodly percentage of the marks will inevitably remain ambiguous and arguable. Still, it is better to try than to totally homogenize and obscure this distinction. The new Barry Cooper edition of the Piano Sonatas, published by the Associated Board in the UK, makes the best attempt that I have seen, whereas in the old Breitkopf Complete Works you will not find even a single stroke.

Who am I to challenge the Beethoven-Haus covey of distinguished scholars on these matters? Well if you don't believe me, recall Beethoven's letter quoted above, and check what Nottebohm says in *Beethoveniana*. His first examples are from the 7th Symphony, showing that Beethoven made numerous corrections which explicitly changed dots to strokes. He then writes, on p. 107: *"To maintain the authenticity of Beethoven's works, we must observe everything he took note of, no matter how trivial it may be, such as the differentiation between strokes and dots."*

So what is the performer to do in the absence of authoritative documentation? Luckily we have access today to a large number of Beethoven manuscript facsimiles, through the website http://imslp. org/. Another site, so far with only a handful of facsimiles, but planning to incorporate many more, is that of the Ira. F. Brilliant Center for Beethoven Studies, at http://mill1.sjlibrary.org:83.

In the absence of reliable information, we should look with skepticism at every published dot or stroke, and experiment with different lengths to see what appeals to our musical instinct. Take this passage from the first movement of the Sonata Op. 81a.

Example 3

Introduction to the Dover Edition

Note that the quarter notes in the first two bars and in the last bar have neither a dot nor a stroke. In this battle between G-flat and F, to play the quarters with strokes very short would introduce a pitiful hiccup into this poignant episode.

In the previously mentioned *Beethoveniana*, Nottebohm has a lengthy article specifically about this conundrum regarding dots and strokes. He reproduces 60 extracts from 26 different works, which demonstrate the distinction between strokes and dots. He concludes that *"one cannot doubt that in Beethoven's works, a note designated with a stroke is meant to be played shorter and more sharply than one with a dot."* Here I part company with him, basing my opinion entirely on evidence from the scores themselves.

Of the 765 articulation marks reproduced in Nottebohm's treatise, 466 are strokes and 299 are dots. Half notes vote 21 – 0 for strokes over dots; sforzatos favor strokes 13 – 0. Indeed, I would be surprised if you could ever find a dot on a sforzato or a half note. As to quarter notes, 163 have strokes and only 9 have dots. But when we get to sixteenth notes, this is reversed, 139 get dots and only 67 have strokes—and those last are mainly isolated notes which clearly want a special accent, like the series of chords interrupted by rests in the Adagio of Op. 31, No.2.

If the stroke is consistently used on longer notes, it is almost unavoidable to conclude that it is indeed longer than the dot. Beethoven's strokes seem to exude an impatient energy that dictates intensity, not extreme shortness. Is it too far-fetched to imagine that as the composer becomes more impassioned in the act of writing, an elongated line, and a heavy one at that, is more satisfying to his emotional state than carefully affixing a fussy, bald dot? Look at the choral entry "Seid Umschlungen, Millionen" in the Finale of the 9th Symphony.

Here Beethoven slashes long heavy strokes above the half notes; they obviously want to be sustained, barely separated; dots could only mislead the performers into a silly caricature of this noble outpouring of joy.

An interesting passage to illuminate this matter is in the cello part of the recapitulation of the 4th Symphony's first movement. Up to this point the leaping, airy motive had always been notated as eighth notes separated by eighth note rests, without any articulation marks. But, in an enlightening slip of the pen, Beethoven suddenly switches in mid-theme to quarter notes with strokes though there is no plausible reason for the length to change at this spot.

So there you have an instant lesson from the composer defining the length of the stroked quarter notes, at least in a rapid tempo, as half of their full value.

In Mozart the question is easier to resolve, partly because he was neater and more consistent than Beethoven, and because he often used dots and strokes differentially in the same theme, as in the opening of the Finale of his Trio in C Major.

This can only sound charming and natural if the strokes are a little longer than the dots. The opposite would sound absurd. In Mozart we often find strokes on half notes, whole notes, and sometimes even on notes tied over to the next bar, which strongly supports the case against their being short. It is unlikely that Mozart's use of strokes would differ greatly from Beethoven's.

Frequently Beethoven omits the dot or stroke from upbeats preceding additional notes of the same value. Considering his obsession with the accuracy of his published works, one cannot imagine that these omissions are unintentional. Notice the very first note in the Sonata Op. 2, No. 1 or in the last movement of the Sonata Op. 10, No. 2.

Even if the shortness of the upbeat were obvious, the aesthetic benefit of seeing the same mark on adjoining notes which are to be played identically should have induced Beethoven to expend the minuscule extra labor of putting in one more dot here and there.

On the other hand, one cannot rule out the possibility that Beethoven might exclaim: *"Idiot! Do I have to indicate every last obvious detail? How can anyone imagine the upbeat would be different from the following short notes?"*

But let us examine the consequences of shortening such upbeats. What if the oboe entrance (and later most of the other instruments) in the last movement of Beethoven's 3rd Piano Concerto adopted this practice?

It would be in absolute contradiction to the piano's opening statement, where the upbeat is actually slurred over.

If the upbeats in this movement are played short, its overwhelming passion and pathos would become flippant and shallow.

Or, look at the solo entrance in Beethoven's First Piano Concerto: playing its upbeat staccato would be as barbaric as playing the dominant chord in the next bar short.

Where he wants staccato, on the eighth note upbeats in the fourth bar, Beethoven does not assume that the performer automatically shortens upbeats, but generously provides the appropriate dots.

Some people maintain that all upbeats in this period were meant to be short. I would suspect and regret every such supposed convention of notation that rules out certain shades of expression. A composer with Beethoven's incredible range of emotions must have the possibility of at least *sometimes* having a long upbeat, even when the following notes are short.

If, indeed, all upbeats are short and light, why then did Beethoven bother to indicate the upbeat stroke in the Menuetto of the same Sonata cited above, Op. 2, No. 1, or at the beginning of the sonatas Op. 2, No. 2 and Op. 10, No. 2, to name just a few?

The Sonata Op. 90 can shed an interesting light on this question.

Introduction to the Dover Edition

In the opening *f* bar, rather than a staccato, Beethoven opts for an eighth followed by a rest. Two bars later, in *p*, it is a full quarter upbeat. Surely this one must be full length.

It is not only on the upbeat that staccatos and strokes are sometimes conspicuously missing in Beethoven. Often it is on the downbeat following a group of staccato notes. A further inspection of the score to the First Piano Concerto reinforces my conviction that Beethoven was very subtle and very conscious about which notes to anoint with a dot. The concerto's opening motive is marked *p*, and ends with a staccato chord.

Example 14

But when the same motive becomes *ff* in the winds, in bar 16 the downbeat is not staccato, and would sound truncated if played very short.

Example 15

Throughout the movement, the analogous downbeats are always marked with a staccato when it is soft, and always without when it is loud.

A similar question is the length of the final note under a short slur. According to some, such notes are also always short. But if indeed the end of a slur is always short (which would put another artificial limitation on musical possibilities), why does Beethoven so often still put a staccato or stroke at the end of a slur? An especially good example is the last movement of the Sonata Op. 31, No. 2, (the "Tempest"), where, on each of its 154 appearances, the four-note slurred motive has a stroke at its end—

Example 16

except at the **ff** climax, the only place where there is also a held, tied-over note above the motive.

Example 17

Can anyone doubt that a distinction is intended here, or believe that Beethoven would have notated those 154 strokes if they were implied anyway by the end of the slur?

In the Finale of the Piano Concerto, No. 3 (See Example 10) shortening the third note would emasculate the theme, giving it three repeated short eighths rather than two. The lower note of that painful diminished 7th must be in the same font as the upper one. Similarly, in the first movement of the Piano Concerto No. 4, clipping the second note of the ubiquitous pairs of eighth notes would utterly destroy its luminous, aristocratic beauty.

Example 18

The variety of lengths desired by Beethoven is beautifully illustrated by the opening run in the Sonata Op. 31, No. 1, which ends with a quarter note.

Example 19

The conventional way to notate the end of a run of sixteenths is not with a quarter, but with an eighth. In the development of this movement Beethoven consistently does exactly that. If he did not intend the quarter note of the opening run to be longer, there would be little point in his writing note values at all. The run can have as much charm with a long ending note as without, provided it is played softly, without any accent. Indeed, that way it nicely balances the even longer opening note.

Introduction to the Dover Edition

Another less frequently occurring puzzle is the question of pairs of tied notes with the fingering 4,3 written above them. If we respect the tie, silently changing fingers on the note might strike some as being a bit precious, and perhaps too petty a detail to bother notating. If on the other hand we repeat the note—no matter how softly—it defeats the intent of the tie. The most famous occurrence of this is in the third movement of the Piano Sonata Op. 110.

It never ceases to amaze (and irritate) me to hear that profound Adagio marred by a senseless deluge of 26 consecutive A-naturals, as though an apprentice piano tuner had hijacked the movement in mid-air.

The best place to start the proof—and one could almost finish there too—is the Scherzo of the A Major Cello Sonata Op. 69.

The piano starts with two quarters tied together over the barline, with that mysterious 4,3 fingering inscribed over them. But 8 bars later the cello echoes the theme, and as the notes are indisputably tied and there is no other indication, every cellist will play it as one note. Surely the two entries are meant to be the same.

Some string players, including Casals, increase the bow speed for the second note, which however sounds more like a tenuto than a repeated note.

Tied notes with the trademark 4,3 fingering over them occur again in the Finale of the Sonata Op. 110, bars 125 and 126; repeating them trivializes this sacred moment to my ears. A similar passage appears in the slow movement of the "Hammerklavier" Sonata.

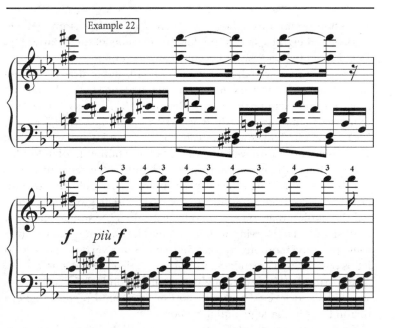

The passage is loud and climactic, and the notes strongly syncopated, serving in effect as a diminution of the longer tied octaves of the preceding bar. To repeat the tied sixteenths here would destroy the syncopation, and with it the dramatic tension. Certainly nobody would even consider repeating the tied octaves.

Shedding further light on these passages are numerous places where Beethoven ties unfingered notes or chords to each other, which could much more easily be written as single notes of longer value. Turning ahead to the next page in the "Hammerklavier," Beethoven went to the labor of notating 38 extra notes (the sixteenths tied to sixteenths) rather than simply writing eighths.

Introduction to the Dover Edition

The same occurs throughout the *Grosse Fuge*, with its innumerable pairs of tied eighths, and in the famous *Cavatina* of the Quartet Op. 130. I don't believe it would occur to anyone to repeat any of these.

Let us return now to the passage in Op. 110, and analyze it rhythmically. Assume for the moment that the tied notes should not be repeated, and examine the effective length of the successive tied notes. Expressed in thirty-seconds the lengths become 6,4,4,3,3,2,2,2,2,2,2,2. Logical, isn't it? The notes gradually speed up until the change of key, after which the last five will slow down because of the ritardando.

If Beethoven did not mean to have such notes repeated, why did he put in his strange fingering? It must indicate a sort of super-tenuto, hold and press against this note to the bitter end, to give at least yourself the illusion that you can thereby make the note sustain and even swell slightly. He is trying to tell us, graphically, rather than writing some pedantic footnote, to treat these notes in a very special way. So let us paraphrase Gertrude Stein, and say: A tie is a tie is a tie!

It is true that Czerny thought that the second of the tied notes should be struck very faintly, as a sort of echo, but I prefer to ignore that in favor of the logic outlined above.

Yet another contentious question, about which it would have been valuable to gather some authentic evidence, is the rhythmic placement of grace notes. Here we must be sure to make a distinction between appoggiaturas, which clearly are to be struck on the beat, and grace notes.

Frequently notes are preceded by a grace note one octave lower. The player seeking erudite authenticity, and knowing well that appoggiaturas must always be on the beat, will perhaps also play such grace notes on the beat. But it can easily be proven that this is not always, if ever, correct. In the Violin Sonata Op. 12, No.1, the fifth and seventh bars have half notes preceded by sixteenth notes an octave (or a seventh) lower.

In the development, the exact same figure is written with grace notes rather than sixteenths.

This "inside evidence" proves that such figures should (at least *sometimes*) be played before the beat; probably they should *never* be on the beat.

As for real appoggiaturas in passages of multiple notes, we need to ask ourselves why the composer wrote them in that manner rather than as regular notes. For example, in the Sonata Op. 10, No. 3, we have a charming, teasing second theme.

It would have been less labor to write four eighth notes than an appoggiatura, a quarter note, and two eighths. Such appoggiaturas must indicate an accent; Beethoven was described by Schindler as always giving special emphasis to dissonant appoggiaturas.

Perhaps the most misunderstood marking in music is "portato"—groups of notes with slurs and dots over them. Again, "inside evidence" provides the clues, as in this passage from the second movement of the String Quartet Op. 59, No. 1,

or in the opening of the slow movement of the Piano Sonata Op. 22.

Introduction to the Dover Edition

Example 28

In both instances the character of the music is smooth and tranquil, short notes would be an assault on this mood. However, the voices with repeated notes cannot be slurred like the other voices, because in Beethoven's time a slur over a pair of repeated notes would have been equivalent to a tie. Note that all the voices which do not have repeated notes are slurred. So we have our answer: portato should be as long and connected as is possible to achieve with repeated notes.

As already stated, the confident artist should always give precedence to artistic instinct rather than slavishly follow ancient (or current!) treatises, which are often dubious, unclear, and in contradiction to each other. Nonetheless, knowledge, as detailed in Kullak's treatise, is never harmful, and ignorance of historical precedents is nothing to be proud of.

If I have not convinced the reader of the validity of my views on some of the perhaps arcane details with which I have dealt, I hope to have at least inspired some thinking about them, and I encourage you to search for your own "inside evidence"!

ANTON KUERTI

Anton Kuerti has performed in recital and with leading orchestras in 40 countries. In Canada he has appeared in 140 communities, and played with every professional orchestra, including 45 concerts with the Toronto Symphony. Kuerti has recorded all of the Beethoven concertos and sonatas, the Brahms and Schumann concertos, and all of the Schubert sonatas, among many other releases. A critic for *Fanfare* wrote that "Kuerti is the best pianist currently playing", and *CD Review* (London) called him "one of the truly great pianists of this century".

Kuerti won the prestigious Leventritt Award when he was still a student. Other awards and honors include numerous honorary doctorates, Officer of the Order of Canada, the Schumann Prize of the Schumann Gesellschaft, and the Governor General's Lifetime Artistic Achievement Award.

Anton Kuerti's CDs can be ordered from www.jwentworth.com/kuerti.

I

GENERAL REMARKS ON BEETHOVEN'S PIANO-PLAYING DOWN TO 1809

The numbers in brackets indicate volume and page of Thayer's Biography,* from which the greater part of this sketch has been taken. All the information concerning Beethoven's improvisation has been utilized only so far as appeared necessary for establishing the connection. More complete details about his piano-playing, down to the period mentioned (1809), may be found in the above biography: I, 114, 120, (163), 164, 208, 213, 237, 283, 381; II, 11, (13), 25, 28, 30, 31, 36, 37, 39, (107), 162, 225, 232, 236, 345 *et seq.*, 355, 363, 409, 411-13; III, 58, 63, 64, 112, (190). Concerning Beethoven's conducting, see II, 352.

LUDWIG VAN BEETHOVEN (born at Bonn, December 16, 1770) received his first instruction in piano-playing and on the violin from his father, the Electoral Court tenor singer, Johann van Beethoven, of Bonn [I, 111]. The latter—perhaps dazzled by the precocious successes of the youthful Mozart, or because frequent pecuniary straits rendered it desirable to turn Ludwig's musical talent to early account—appears to have urged his son, at a tender age, to severe piano-practice. Consequently, as early as March 26, 1778 (as per *avertissement*), if not even earlier, the latter was in a position to " have the honour to execute divers concertos at the Hall of the Musical Academy in the *Sternengass* [a street] " [II, 408-9]. In his ninth year, or thereabouts, his instruction was confided to the tenor singer (former musical director and oboist) Tobias Friedrich Pfeiffer, who is described as a finished pianist [I, 114, 344, 70], until P.'s departure from Bonn, *i.e.*, for about one year. On the organ he was taught by van den Eeden, about 1780. In later years Beethoven " often conversed with Schindler about the aged organist,

* " Life of Ludwig van Beethoven," by Alexander Wheelock Thayer. Edition in German, after the original manuscript, by H. Deiters in Bonn (according to the Preface).—Vol. I: Berlin, Ferdinand Schneider, 1866.—Vol. II: Berlin, W. Weber, 1872.—Vol. III (down to the year 1816): Berlin, do., 1879. The conclusion has not yet (1900) appeared.

when discussing the characteristic position and movement of the body and hands in playing the organ and piano; he had been taught, he said, that the motions of both body and hands should be *quiet* and *measured*" * [I, 114].

Van den Eeden was followed, about 1781, by Christian Gottlob Neefe "as Beethoven's music-teacher" [I, 117]. Neefe, himself "a zealous disciple of the Bach † school," instructed the boy both in thorough-bass and composition.

Touching the achievements of his pupil as a pianist, at that time, "Cramer's Magazine" ‡ reports: "He plays the piano with vigor and in a finished style, is a very good sight-reader, and (to say all in a word) plays chiefly 'The Well-tempered Clavichord,' by Sebastian Bach, which was put into his hands by Herr Neefe" [I, 120]. When Neefe left Bonn temporarily, on June 20, 1782, Ludwig, now nearly twelve years old, was able to take his place on the organ-bench. Next year he was still further advanced; Beethoven became "cembalist in the orchestra," having to lead the operatic performances at the piano. Hence his early familiarity with scores, and consequent virtuosity in reading and playing from them [I, 122]. Thayer ascribes to the following year, 1784, the composition of "Un Concert pour le Clavecin ou Forte-piano, composé par Louis van Beethoven, agé de douze [!] ans" (unpublished) [I, 128], to which we also refer in our introduction to the C-major Concerto.

In the spring of 1787 Beethoven made a trip to Vienna, where he had some lessons from Mozart; "but Beethoven complained that the latter *never played to him*" § [Ries: "Notizen," p. 86]. These were probably lessons in composition [I, 163 *et seq.*]. Soon returning to Bonn, in 1788 we find Beethoven in a new field of activity; he took a position as viola-player in the court orchestra, consisting of thirty-one

---

* The editor has taken the liberty of *italicizing* statements of peculiar interest in the present sketch.

† "Formed in the strict Leipzig school" [I, 119].

‡ Very likely inspired by Neefe himself (?).

§ Nevertheless, Beethoven must have heard him, if one of our following notes is based on fact.

pieces, conducted by Reicha [I, 183], retaining this place until 1792 ; that is, until his definitive removal to Vienna.   Meantime, he doubtless did not neglect the piano ;   " Herr Ludwig van Beethoven plays piano-forte-concertos, and Herr Neefe accompanies at court, in the theatre, and in concerts," says " Bossler's Musical Correspondence " for July 13, 1791 [Thayer: I, 204].   That autumn we meet Beethoven, with other members of the orchestra, and actors and singers, on their way to Mergentheim [I, 205 *et seq.*].   They proceeded *via* Aschaffenburg-on-Main, the home of Abbé Sterkel, " one of the foremost pianists in all Germany " [207].   " Beethoven," narrates Wegeler [" Notizen," p. 17], " who had never before heard a great, illustrious pianist,* *was unfamiliar with the fine shadings* [?] in the treatment of the instrument ; his playing was rough and hard."   Nevertheless, when requested to play his variations on " Vieni, Amore," he performed " not only these variations, so far as he could remember them, .   .   .   but also a great many others, not less difficult, and, to the extreme surprise of his audience, in precise and *perfect imitation of the elegant style* which had impressed him in Sterkel's playing " [!] [Th., I, 208].   In Mergentheim Beethoven did not play in public :   " Perhaps [so says the benevolent reporter Carl Ludwig Junker, chaplain at Kirchberg, in " Bossler's Musical Correspondence "] because he found the instrument unsuitable ; it was a Spath grand, and he is accustomed, in Bonn, to play only on a Stein grand.   However, what I infinitely preferred, I heard him improvise " ; and thereby he measures " the greatness in virtuosity of this amiable, finely organized man " ; he even compares him with the celebrated Abbé Vogler (the teacher of Meyerbeer and Weber), whom he had " frequently heard, for hours together " ; but " Bethoven," to his mind, is, " aside from his dexterity, *more eloquent, imposing, expressive—in a word, touches the heart more ; he is, there-fore, as fine in Adagio as in Allegro* " ; he is likewise " so modest, so wholly unassuming.   And still he admitted, that on the journeys which the Elector permitted him to undertake, he had seldom found, among the best-known pianists of distinction, what he had felt justified in

* And Mozart ?—He died on December 5th of the same year.

expecting. Indeed, *his playing differs so greatly from the usual method of treating the piano*, that it seems as if he had struck out an *entirely new path* for himself, in order to reach the goal of perfection to which he has attained" [I, 213]. These words show that Beethoven was already at the end of his pianistic "apprenticeship." On his arrival, in November, 1792, at Vienna, thenceforward his permanent dwelling-place, his most immediate care was to finish his studies in theory and composition. For two and one-half years the young artist, whom Neefe called, in 1793, "now unquestionably one of the foremost pianists" [I, 227], devoted himself to these studies, before appearing in Vienna (as far as we now know) for the first time as a player and as the composer of a piano-concerto [compare our Introduction to the C-major Concerto], in which capacities, according to the "Vienna Gazette" of April 1, 1795, he won "the unanimous applause of the audience" [Nottebohm : "Musikalisches Wochenblatt," Vol. VI, No. 48].

Before accompanying Beethoven in his subsequent artistic career, it will be of interest to learn his own opinion on Mozart's playing—the more so because the partisans of Mozart form no inconsiderable contingent of his later critics.

"Beethoven told Czerny that he had heard Mozart play ; his execution was delicate, but choppy, without *legato* [?], a style of which the first admirable master was B., who treated the piano like an organ" [II, 409].

Similarly runs a passage from Czerny's correspondence with Cocks in London : "Beethoven, who had heard Mozart play,* said afterwards that his playing was neat and clear, but rather empty, weak, and old-fashioned.† The *legato* and *cantabile* on the piano were unknown at

---

* According to our preceding remarks, it seems most probable that this happened at the time when Beethoven himself played before Mozart (1787). To be sure, Ries's note contradicts this ; however, B. says only, that Mozart did not play to him, *i.e.*, to him alone, during lesson-time.

† On the other hand, Beethoven very highly esteemed Mozart as a composer. "Of all composers [says Ries, "Notizen," p. 84], Beethoven thought most highly of Mozart and Händel, Seb. Bach following" [Th., II, 345]. Of Bach's works he possessed, however, but a small collection [Schindler, II, 184].

that time,* and B. was the first to discover [these?] new and grand effects on that instrument" [II, 363].

While Beethoven may thus have criticized Mozart's playing, the partisans of Mozart had their own opinion concerning *his* playing. It is reflected in a communication of Mosel's (a "competent critic"), in Schmidt's "Wiener Musikzeitung" of October 18, 1843, and reads [acc. to Thayer, II, 39] thus: "A year after the appearance of 'The Magic Flute,' a star of the first magnitude rose above Vienna's musical horizon. Beethoven came hither, and attracted general attention as a pianist even then. We had already lost Mozart; all the more welcome, therefore, was a new and so admirable artist on the same instrument. True, an important difference was apparent in the style of these two; the roundness, tranquillity, and delicacy of Mozart's style were foreign to the new virtuoso; on the other hand, his enhanced vigor and fiery expression affected every listener. . . ."

"In the year 1798," narrates Tomaschek, "Beethoven, the giant among pianists, came to Prague. He gave a well-attended concert, at which he played his C-major Concerto, op. 15. I felt myself strangely thrilled by the grandeur of Beethoven's playing, and more especially by the daring flight of his conceptive fancy. . . . In his second concert, his playing and compositions did not have the same overpowering effect upon me; this time he executed the concerto in B♭-major. I heard him for a third time at Count C.'s, where, besides playing the graceful Rondo from the A-major Sonata, he improvised on the theme, 'À vous dirai-je, Maman?'; though admiring his vigorous and brilliant playing, his frequent bold digressions from one motive to another did not escape me," etc. [II, 29].

In the same measure as Beethoven's creative genius continually sought greater and loftier tasks, his careful attention to the details of technique appears to have relaxed. Yet, at this period, there was no

* " The animation of the Allegro is usually expressed in staccato notes, and the tenderness of the Adagio in sustained and slurred notes," says Ph. E. Bach in his "Essay on the True Mode of Playing the Clavier" (Third Ed., Leipzig, 1787, Chapter III, " On Style," §5). Therefore, the above observation is by no means to be taken literally.

lack of inducement to him to keep green his laurels as a player, as well. He now found a formidable rival in Joseph Wölffl, of Salzburg. "It was like a revival," says Ignaz von Seyfried, "of the old Parisian feud between the Gluckists and Piccinnists; and the many lovers of art in the imperial capital split into two parties. But this rivalry did not prevent the two artists from seating themselves side by side at two pianos and alternately improvising on themes proposed by one to the other. . . . It would be hard, perhaps impossible, to award the palm of victory in mechanical dexterity to either champion; to Wölffl, Mother Nature had been peculiarly kind in giving him a gigantic hand which stretched tenths as easily as other players' hands take octaves, so that he could play running passages in tenths at a tremendous pace. In improvisation, Beethoven's characteristic of weird gloominess was already in evidence; Wölffl, on the other hand, trained in Mozart's school, was always equable; never shallow, but always clear, and for that very reason more accessible to the majority. Whoever has heard Hummel will understand what this means." [II, 27.]

Wölffl's outward success is also intimated by the reporter for the "Leipziger Allgemeine Musikalische Zeitung" of April 22, 1799: "Opinions differ here as to the superiority of the one over the other; but it seems as if the larger party inclined to the side of the latter [Wölffl]; Beethoven's playing is extremely brilliant, but less delicate, and at times falls into indistinctness. Wölffl, of course, gains especially by his unpretentious, obliging deportment, in contrast with Beethoven's rather lofty manner." [II, 25.]

Beethoven met with a still more dangerous "rival" in J. B. Cramer, who (according to Thayer) "at the beginning of our century was, for a number of years, on the whole the foremost of European pianists." He "excelled Beethoven in the perfect cleanness and correctness of his interpretation; Beethoven assured him that he preferred his touch to that of any other player. His technique was astounding; but he distinguished himself in a yet higher degree by taste, feeling, and expression. But Beethoven ranked far above him in force and energy, especially when improvising" [II, 35 *et seq.*]. Beethoven's opinion of

Cramer is corroborated by Ries : " Among pianists he praises only one as an excellent player—John Cramer. Of all the rest he thought little." Concerning Beethoven, Cramer himself said long afterward : " All in all, Beethoven was, if not the greatest, certainly one of the greatest and most admirable pianists that he had ever heard, both as regards expression and dexterity " [acc. to Mr. Appleby's statement, Th., II, 36].

Such associations and stimuli would appear to have been not without influence on Beethoven himself. " I have also greatly perfected my piano-playing," he writes to Amenda in 1801 [Th., II, 23 and 137]. Of the A♭-major Sonata, op. 26, Czerny observes that the Finale is an intentional reminiscence of the Clementi-Cramer running style of Finale * [II, 134].

Cramer heard him in 1799–1800 ; Cherubini, in 1805–6, when his deafness was already increasing. Schindler, who discussed Beethoven's playing with both, at the beginning of the forties, reports as follows : " Cherubini, in his unceremonious way, characterized it in one word as ' rough.' Cramer, the gentleman, found fault less with the roughness of his execution than with his uncertainty in the interpretation of one and the same composition—to-day spirited and full of characteristic expression, to-morrow eccentric to indistinctness, often confused " [Th., II, 37]. We have already hinted at the reason of this " indistinctness," and shall meet further on with direct statements concerning it. And here let us note, from Schindler's " Biography " [Third Ed., II, 232], Clementi's opinion on Beethoven the pianist, as expressed to the author in 1827 : " His playing was but little cultivated, not seldom violent, like himself, but always full of spirit." As late as 1807, Clementi heard Beethoven play several compositions in Vienna.

At the present time there are three points of view from which a pianistic performance is usually criticized : Technique, Style, Touch. However subjective the above criticisms may be, their consensus of opinion shows that Beethoven's style was admirable, that his technique was fully abreast of the time, and—a point which nowadays requires

* A further " Reminiscence" is probably found in the Finale of the F-major Sonata, op. 54.

peculiar emphasis—that he possessed a forceful touch. Possibly he sometimes exaggerated this last; either passionate irritation, or insufficient preparation, may have led him to extremes; but, possibly, the ears of his critics were pampered.

．　．　．　．　．　．　．

Toward the end of 1800 Czerny, then nine years old, introduced himself to Beethoven. At this early age Czerny was already such a finished pianist that he ventured to appear for the first time in public with Mozart's C-minor Concerto. He now played, before Beethoven, the aforesaid master's C-major Concerto (*œuvre posthume*), "in the accompaniment-passages of which Beethoven himself filled in the melody with his left hand; also other pieces. Beethoven expressed himself graciously and favorably regarding the boy's talents, and offered to take him as a pupil. He taught him at first after Emanuel Bach's 'Klavierschule,' and, later, instructed him in the interpretation of most of his own compositions which had appeared in print." Czerny stated that this instruction was chiefly directed to style [Th., II, 107].

A chief incentive for the present writer to consult Thayer's "Biography," while editing the Beethoven Concertos, was the desire to obtain the clearest evidence possible concerning the relation of Czerny—this oft-impeached, yet perhaps most important witness—to Beethoven. Czerny says of himself, in his "Art of Style" (p. 32, note), "that as early as 1801 he began to take lessons of Beethoven, taking up for study all his works immediately on publication, and many of them under the master's own supervision, with great predilection; and that in later years, as well, until near Beethoven's end, he had enjoyed friendly and instructive intercourse with him." On December 7, 1805, Beethoven gave the boy a brilliant testimonial; but warned him, on the other hand, not to make too free use of his extraordinary memory, because he would lose, "by so doing, the power of swift, comprehensive survey and sight-reading, and also miss here and there the correct accentuation" [Th., II, 298].*

* "Czerny has no legato, and accents wrongly"—such (acc. to Schindler, "Biography," III, 236) was Beethoven's repeated censure (from 1818–20 ?).

Beethoven's Piano Playing

Schindler ["Biography," II, p. 235] extols Czerny's services in hindering, for some years, the disappearance of Beethoven's compositions from the repertory in Vienna. "The fact," he says, "is no less indisputable, that Czerny was the only one among the Viennese virtuosi who took the pains to hear Beethoven often during his prime. He is, therefore, deserving of consideration down to the point when he begins to improve Beethoven's compositions with additions of modern virtuosity."

These "additions" were:

(1) Transportation of the *cantilena* from the one- and two-lined octaves into the three- and four-lined octaves.

(2) Employment of trills and other graces.

(3) Exaggerated use of the pedal.

(4) Metronomic regulation.

Touching points 1 and 2, Czerny himself, in his "Art of Style," expresses himself in a sense diametrically opposite. As to the use of the pedal in Beethoven's works, we shall quote directly a note of decided interest; and as to point 4, it is Nottebohm's opinion ["Beethoveniana," Leipzig and Winterthur: 1872; Metronomic Markings, p. 136] that Czerny's metronome-marks (in the "Art of Style,") "if not of authentic validity, yet have some claim on our confidence," particularly in the case of works of which we know that Czerny either heard Beethoven play them, or studied them under his direction. "Whoever (he says) knew C. Czerny personally, and had opportunity to study his peculiarly practical temperament, would feel confidence in his ability to impress firmly on his memory the tempo of a piece which he had heard, and would have observed the sureness which he manifested in seizing on such externals of music."

Now, as the following statements of Czerny's relate principally to such "externals of music," we shall be able to feel all the more confidence in them, as they contain, in a high degree, internal probability of their trustworthiness.

After giving very interesting information on the form of Beethoven's

improvisations, for the details of which consult Thayer [II, 347],*
Czerny continues thus: "In the swiftness of his scales, double trills,
leaps, etc., no one, not even Hummel, rivalled him. His attitude in
playing was masterly in its tranquillity and refinement, without the
slightest gesticulation (except bending over as his deafness increased);
his fingers were very strong, not long, and broadened at the tips by
much playing.

"In teaching, too, he insisted on a correct position of the fingers
according to Em. Bach's method, by which he instructed me; he himself could hardly [?] stretch a tenth. He used the pedal a great deal,
far more than is indicated in his works. His interpretation of Händel's
and Gluck's scores, and of Seb. Bach's fugues, was unique; the first-
named he reproduced with a fullness of harmony and a spirit which
transformed these compositions.

"Extraordinary as was his playing in improvisation, it was often less
satisfactory in the execution of his already engraved compositions; for,
as he never had patience or time to practise anything, his success in
interpretation depended chiefly on chance and mood; besides, his
playing, as well as his compositions, being in advance of his period, his
titanic execution was too much for the pianofortes then made, which
(up to 1810) were very weak and incomplete. Hence it came that
Hummel's pearly and brilliant style, so well adapted to the times, was,
of course, much more intelligible and attractive to the general public.
But Beethoven's playing of the Adagio and Legato in the strict style
exercised a wellnigh magic influence on every hearer, and has never, so
far as I know, been surpassed by any one" [Th., II, 348].

Another pupil of Beethoven, Ferdinand Ries (b. 1784), came late
in the autumn of 1801 to Vienna [II, 163], then studying until the

---

* But without allowing oneself to be led into wasting too much time on imita-
tions! Fortunately, public improvisations, which, however great the composer's
gifts may be, never attain the value of well-considered and thoroughly worked-out
compositions, have now wellnigh gone out of fashion. For the rest, most of the
Beethoven Cadenzas bear the character of improvisations, whereas those to the
B♭-major Concerto—probably the best of them all—appear to have been more
carefully worked out.

year 1805 under Beethoven [II, 273]. At the end of August, 1808, he returned for a prolonged visit (about ten months) to Vienna [III, 47], later going to England. He was the first to appear in public as Beethoven's pupil, this being in July, 1804, at the "Augarten," where he played Beethoven's C-minor Concerto, and was highly praised [II, 256-7]. Czerny, who often played with him at a second piano, says of him: "Ries played with finished execution, but coldly" [II, 16]. The following of his (Ries's) observations are of special interest to us:

"I can remember only two cases in which Beethoven told me that I should add a few notes to his compositions; once in the Rondo to the *Sonate pathétique* (op. 13), and the other time to the theme of the Rondo in his first Concerto in C major,* where he directed me to play several double notes to render it more brilliant.† Altogether, he played this Rondo with unique expression. In general, he himself played his compositions most eccentrically, though usually keeping strict time, only occasionally hurrying the tempo somewhat. Sometimes he would play a *crescendo* with a *ritardando*, which made a very fine and striking effect. In playing he would give, now to one passage and again to another, in the right hand or left, a beautiful, fairly inimitable expression; but he very rarely indeed added notes or a grace"‡ [II, 346].

We can discern Beethoven's chief aim in the interpretation of his compositions from Ries's description of his lessons [*cf.* Th., II, 165].

* *Cf.* our note on this passage.

† With regard to alterations, Schindler says ["Biogr.," II, 252] very bitterly, that the difference between Czerny and Ries was simply this: "that Czerny had for years carried on his practices practically under the master's eye, and theoretically after the latter's death; whereas Ries had made the statement concerning Beethoven's music, in London and other places, that the changes which he made were in accordance with the master's intentions." But Czerny requires, theoretically, "no alterations at all"; and Ries, in point of fact, can remember only two cases. How does this agree with Schindler's reproaches? (But *cf.* "Biogr.," II, 155.)

‡ "So, that is right—sing it so, . . . and don't put in a 'mortant,'" said Beethoven to the youthful singer, Fräulein Adamberger (according to her own account), while teaching her to sing the songs in "Egmont" [Th., III, 136].

In his case, as before, the master's attention was directed principally to style. "When I (says Ries) made a mistake in a passage, or struck wrongly notes or leaps which he often wanted specially emphasized, he seldom said anything; but if my fault was in expression, or a crescendo, etc., or in the character of the piece, he became angry, because, as he said, the former was accidental, while the latter showed a lack of knowledge, feeling, or attention. He himself very often made mistakes of the former kind, even when playing in public" [II, 165].

In the latter part of this period, as observed above, Beethoven's pianistic achievements were already on the wane. Whether the not wholly satisfactory performance of the C-minor Concerto at the concert given on April 5, 1803, was partly due to external circumstances,* or whether increasing deafness was partly to blame for the deterioration in Beethoven's playing—at all events, he no longer had inclination or time for technical practice. Even in private circles (as Thayer learns from Seyfried), "it required manifold and repeated urging, when he was not just in the humor, merely to get him to the piano." † True, he still appeared in public, for the last time in 1814 [Th., III, 277 *et seq.*] ;‡ but as early as February, 1812, Carl Czerny was entrusted with the first public production of Beethoven's last piano-concerto in E♭ (comp. 1809), and in concerts given in more private circles he (Beethoven) had long since made way for the Baroness Ertmann [Th., III, 190].

On his pupils devolved the task of interpreting and popularizing the piano-works of their master. "Once [before 1805?] (says Ries :

* Ries was called to Beethoven at five o'clock that morning ! He found him at work writing out the trombone parts to the oratorio, "Christ on the Mount of Olives," which was also to be given. At eight o'clock began the "terrible" rehearsal ; at half-past two "all were exhausted" and more or less dissatisfied. After a lunch, ordered by Prince Karl Lichnowsky, the oratorio was rehearsed again. At six the concert commenced—Beethoven's first two symphonies, the piano-concerto, and the oratorio. On account of the length of the concert, a few other pieces were omitted [Ries, "Notizen," p. 76 *et seq.;* Th., II, 224 *et seq.*]. By that time the pianist might well be "exhausted" !

† Before he began to play, he used to strike the keys with the palm of his hand ; to draw a finger swiftly across them—in short, to play all kinds of tricks, at which he himself laughed heartily, as was his wont [Th., II, 355].

‡ Twice, with the B♭-major Trio, op. 97.

'Notizen,' p. 100) he seriously set about planning a grand tour with me, in which I was to arrange all the concerts, and to play his piano-concertos and other compositions. He himself intended to conduct, and only to improvise." The real close of his career as a virtuoso was the " grosse Akademie " [grand concert] of December 22, 1808, at which Beethoven publicly performed his Fourth Concerto and the Fantasia with Chorus (for the first time). The correspondent of the Leipzig " Allg. Mus. Zeitung " calls the performance of this concert " defective in every respect " [III, 58]. It lasted from 6.30 to 10.30 ! Besides the above piano-works, the Pastorale and the C-minor Symphonies, and other pieces, " all entirely new," were produced. As to the execution of the G-major Concerto, Reichard writes : " A new fortepiano-concerto of prodigious difficulty, which Beethoven played with astounding clever-ness in the fastest possible *tempis* [sic]. The Adagio, a masterly move-ment of beautifully developed song, he positively made to sing on his instrument, with a deep, melancholy feeling that thrilled me, as well " [Th., *ibid.*].

About this time, Friedrich Nisle, the horn-virtuoso and composer, also heard him. Describing his visit to B. (in the Berlin " Allg. Mus. Zeitung," 1829), after a portrayal of Beethoven's improvising, he con-tinues : " I was told that Beethoven has pupils in Vienna, *who play his pieces better than he himself*. I could not forbear smiling. As a player he is, to be sure, inferior to many others in elegance and technical accomplishments ; besides, being hard of hearing, he played rather loud. But one lost sight of these defects when the master disclosed the depths of his soul. And can fashionable taste, or dexterity (which often sinks to empty finger-bravura), compensate for the absence of a Beethovenish soul?—Ah, my dear people, methought, pray take to heart, at last, what our great Teacher said so many hundred years ago : ' *The spirit giveth life.*' " [Th., III, 63.]

II

GENERAL RULES FOR THE PERFORMANCE OF THE BEET-HOVEN PIANOFORTE-CONCERTOS

In Carl Czerny's " Kunst des Vortrags " ("Art of Style "; supplement to the great Pianoforte-Method, op. 500), which is continually cited in establishing and comparing the tempi of the concertos, Chapters II and III contain directions "for the correct performance of all Beethoven's piano-works for piano-solo and with accompaniment." *

These directions consist of discussions of the several works, or rather movements; of metronomic markings, details concerning the conception of important passages, occasional fingerings, other practical hints, etc., etc., the validity of which we shall not, at present, examine in detail. We shall, however, give brief consideration to the General Rules laid down by the author in the introductory paragraphs of Chapter II and the closing observations of Chapter III.

We read in Chapter II, § 8 :

" In the performance of his works (and in classical compositions in general) the player must not allow himself to make any alteration of the composition, any addition, or any abbreviation whatever."

The general applicability of this dictum can hardly be disputed. However, the omission of certain reprises in familiar sonatas and chamber-compositions cannot well be regarded as a censurable exception.†

* Published in Vienna by A. Diabelli & Co. In Nottebohm's " Thematic Catalogue," Chapters II and III are also given as separately printed (Vienna : Spina).

† Indeed, Schindler narrates (Biography, 3d ed., Vol. II, p. 215) that Beethoven, prompted by the project (1823) for a complete edition of his works, "considered whether, in order to attain greater unity, he should not transform some of his earlier four-movement sonatas, in which the number of movements merely conformed

And although Ries says that Beethoven directed him to add a few notes to the Rondo of the C-major Concerto, " to make it more brilliant," the composer most undoubtedly had a right to do so; but for us, in this matter, Czerny's rule must be adhered to.

" Also in the case of piano-pieces of the earlier period, which were written for the five-octave instruments then in use, the attempt to employ additional notes in the sixth octave has always resulted unfavorably, and all, even the apparently most tasteful embellishments, etc., not indicated by the author himself, are rightly regarded as superfluous. For one wishes to hear the work of art in its original form, as conceived and penned by the master."

While Czerny was writing these lines, he very probably remembered a concert in the year 1816, at which, during his performance of Beethoven's quintet with wind-instruments, he permitted himself (" with juvenile levity ") certain alterations, consisting of " more complicated passages, the employment of the higher octave, etc.," which earned him Beethoven's censure in the presence of the other executants [Th., III, 381]. (Schindler, on the other hand, writes concerning another projected edition of that same year [1816], that one reason " for a new edition of the pianoforte-works was derived from the extension of the keyboard then attained," and points out certain passages in the sonatas, op. 2 and 10. " It is evident, that in many works not merely the alteration of a few notes is required, but that entire passages have to be rewritten, a more formidable task in the case of polyphonic works, the concertos and others, than in the sonatas for pianoforte solo." [Th., III, 380.]) It seems to the present editor, that in many cases one need not hesitate to employ the contra-octave, or to double the lower bass notes in octave-passages whose downward tendency is abruptly checked by a lack of the tones below contra-*F*. But any, even well-motivated, alterations in the treble demand extreme delicacy and caution. Finally, facilitations dictated by physical deficiencies (*e.g.*,

to common usage, into three-movement pieces. He had, however, declared positively only for the excision of the ' Scherzo allegro ' from the highly pathetic sonata with violin, op. 30 in C minor, as being at variance with the general character of the work."

too small hands) may, when they do not disturb the fundamental idea of the given passage, also be classed among alterations to be tolerated. But players should thoughtfully consider whether such deficiencies do, in reality, permit them to embrace a public career as pianists.*

Still more important than these introductory rules is the "Closing Remark" in Chapter III, §33:

On the Intellectual Apprehension of Beethoven's Compositions.

"In general, in the case of a rôle represented by several good actors (*e.g.*, "Hamlet"), the conception of each will differ in various details from that of all the rest; one will give special prominence to his melancholy, another to his irony, a third to his pretence of madness, etc. And yet each of these presentations may be wholly satisfactory in its kind, if only the main idea be correct.

"In the performance, too, of classical compositions, more particularly those by Beethoven, much depends on the individuality of the player. (In all cases, of course, we take for granted a certain degree of virtuosity; for a bungler can never dream of intellectual conception.)

"Thus the one may lay most stress on humor, a second on seriousness, a third on emotion, a fourth on bravura (!) ; but he who unites them all is assuredly the best.

---

* Have our piano-makers, in point of fact, hit the true keyboard-span for the octave? In our opinion, the stretch of a tenth so often required in Beethoven's piano-works ought to be entirely practicable for hands of medium size. See, for instance, the Adagio of op. 106, where a careful distinction is made between

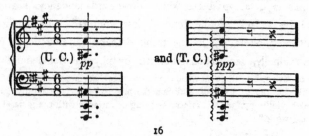

" There are, however, material requirements which are absolutely essential, and upon which all else depends, namely :

" (1) The correct tempo.

" (2) The exact observance of all expression-marks, which Beethoven (particularly in his later works) set down with great precision.

" (3) A complete command of all difficulties, and the development of a good style in every respect upon the basis of careful study of other composers," etc.

Although these remarks will hardly bear strict logical scrutiny, we readily perceive what is intended. Nevertheless, we feel bound to add that any interpretation of a Beethoven composition will, in fact, take on a more or less subjective coloring, according to the talent and stage of development of the player; and we, too, shall not withhold our approbation "if only the main idea be correct." In reality, however, there can be, for any composition, only one correct conception—the conception which the composer had of his work while creating it.*
True, this conception will remain, for the time being, only an ideal one ; but let us hope that musical talent, united with imagination and refinement of feeling, can succeed (and has succeeded) in penetrating into the character of a Beethoven composition, and from this standpoint to reconstruct the ideal, or at least to approach it as closely as possible. To this end various other means will assist us—such as an acquaintance with the finest works of his predecessors, and also with as many as possible of those among his own works which precede the one in question, besides traditions, opinions, etc. So-called traditions must, however, be carefully weighed. Cramer early criticized, in Beethoven's playing, the " uneven reproduction of one and the same composition " ; and what differences may have resulted from the further development of his later

* Or, more exactly, that conception which completely coincides with the idea of the work ; for who could disprove an assertion that the composer, in consequence of unremitting mental work, may (for instance) have ended by imagining too rapid tempi for his movements ? But these are speculations which would carry us too far. Here we have to do with the contrast between " the composer's intentions " and "subjective conception," whether deriving from external influences or from changes in the mood or the art-conception of the author himself.

years! Even in the case of statements derived from the personal teachings of the composer, we must not forget that we receive them only through the medium of a third person.

Among the material requirements for a correct conception, Czerny rightly places the tempo in the first rank. Nothing can so greatly affect the character of a piece of music as a mistake in this particular. For the editor, at least, the audition of an overhastened Allegro or a dragging Adagio is one of the worst of musical tortures. The tempo finds most precise expression in the metronome-mark.

"We have endeavored," writes Czerny (Chap. III, §34), "according to the best of our recollection, to correctly indicate the tempo, this most important part of a correct conception."

In the first part of this sketch we already mentioned Czerny's extraordinary memory, and also spoke of the (not wholly unlimited) confidence reposed by Nottebohm in Czerny's metronomic markings—at least in the case of works which he studied with, or heard played by, Beethoven. (*Cf.* p. 8, preceding.) We are aware, on the other hand, that Schindler reckoned among the "additions of the modern virtuoso," wherewith Czerny desired to "improve" Beethoven's compositions, these same metronomic markings. Schindler considered the Beethoven performances of other famous artists too swift. It is probable, therefore, that his condemnation is referable rather to a hasty denunciation of the "additions" in general than to Czerny's metronomic markings in particular. For he must have known that Beethoven himself provided his Symphonies with metronome-marks.

To the best of his recollection the present editor, in most cases, fixed the metronomization of the Concertos independently, and then compared the several movements with Czerny's. In the great majority of cases, and after mature consideration, he found it advisable to deviate but very little from Czerny's tempi; and any such deviations seemed needful only for the attainment of greater plasticity. A difference of a very few degrees on the metronome can, in any event, lead to no material differences in the tempo, such as could be found fault with in either direction. On the other hand, the editor found Czerny's metronomization of the first movement in both the earliest concertos decidedly too fast. For the sake of clearness we give below Czerny's markings for the first movements of all five concertos:

			(Czerny.)
Fourth Concerto		Allegro moderato	$\quad = 116.$
Fifth	"	Allegro	$\quad = 132.$
Third	"	Allegro con brio	$\quad = 144.$
Second	"	" " "	$\quad = 152.$
First	"	" " "	$\quad = 88$ (*i.e.*, $\quad = 176$).

In the Fourth Concerto we quite agreed with Czerny; in the Fifth the tempo appeared to us "a trifle" too lively; in the Third, also, we deviated but slightly ($\quad = 138$). But the metronomization of the first movement of the Second Concerto appeared to us too rapid. Here the shadings with which certain passages are provided, form a criterion of the rapidity which should not be too lightly estimated. True, passages like the following:

may be distinctly executed, even with the staccatos, at "$\quad = 152$," but in that case demand a degree of virtuosity quite out of proportion to the other difficulties of the Concerto.

But the metronomization of the First Concerto struck us as decidedly wrong. Czerny's intention is apparent from the added remarks; the Concerto was evidently too easy for him, and he therefore demands that an appearance of bravura should be given the passages, in themselves not at all difficult, by a "brilliant" touch. Aside from this, however, he manifestly transformed the C-time to *alla-breve* time by the marking "$\quad = 88$." To be sure, he could hardly have marked it $\quad = 176$, because the higher figures were obviously not given on his metronome. Its inventor, perhaps correctly surmising that swifter fractions of time than 160 to the minute would not be required for fixing the tempo, extended his scale only to that figure. [Still (acc. to Schindler: Biogr., 3rd ed., II, p. 249), "as early as the twenties" he had metronomes made by his brother in Vienna, with a scale of 40–208.] Beating time to quarter-notes at 172 would doubtless result in comical gesticulation. But this does not affect the matter in hand. "$\math>{\flat} = 88$" is *alla-breve* time, which we are unable to recognize in the first movement of the C-major Concerto. Apart from the frequent passages in sixteenth-notes, the first theme does *not* bear a *bipartite* character:

But what will our readers say when we confess that even this immoderate tempo ($\mathscr{d} = 88$) appears discreet in comparison with those which Beethoven himself gave for the metronomization of the Allegro movements of his Symphonies? In them there is not one simple Allegro (**C**) measured by quarter-notes; Allegro **C** does not begin until $\mathscr{d} = 80$; among the *Allegro con brio* movements there is but one in $\frac{4}{4}$ time, $\mathscr{d} = 100$; an *Allegro ma non tanto* (in the Ninth Symphony) has **¢**, $\mathscr{d} = 120$; and among the *Allegro vivace* movements in **¢** one even goes as high as $\mathscr{o} = 84$, *i.e.*, $\mathscr{d} = 168$. Compared with these, Czerny's tempi are mere child's play.

But let us examine the two Allegro movements more closely. One of them, $\mathscr{d} = 84$, is the Finale of the C-minor Symphony. Despite its time-signature **C**, we must concede that it may far more properly be regarded as an alla-breve movement than the Allegro of the First Concerto (acc. to Czerny).

The principal passages are formed of eighth-notes and triplets of eighth-notes; sixteenth-notes appear only as tremolo, as small fluttering figures, or in short scale-like passages. In view of these conditions, the tempo is really very moderate.

The other movement is the thunderstorm Allegro in the Pastoral Symphony (**C**, $\textstyle\unicode{x1D15F} = 80$). This is likewise to be considered alla-breve time; the tempo-mark is, possibly, too simply expressed.

However, touching these symphony-tempi in general, Nottebohm says ("Metronomische Bezeichnungen," Beethoveniana, p. 135): "The metronomization of some symphony-movements, in particular, strikes us as too rapid"; and: "Concerning the very rapid marking of the last movement of the Fourth Symphony (Allegro ma non troppo, $\textstyle\unicode{x1D15F} = 80$), a mistake may be assumed."

How it happens that the metronomization, by the composer himself, "of some symphony-movements" appears too rapid, is hard to explain. For fixing metronome-marks there is requisite, above all, patience and inner tranquillity. When Beethoven published the metronomic markings of his first eight symphonies in a little pamphlet,* Mälzel's Metronome had been known but a short time (Nottebohm says, from about 1815). Long practice in its manipulation can, therefore, not be assumed in Beethoven's case. Besides, who knows whether it may not happen that composers themselves involuntarily set their tempi too high, either to render them more brilliant, or from apprehension that their "fire" might otherwise be dulled ?

* "Symphonien No. 1-8 und Septett von dem Autor selbst bezeichnet"; Steiner & Co., 1817. [Nottebohm, as above, p. 130.]

21

With reference to the Ninth Symphony, Schindler [Biogr., II, 250] gives an anecdote which is highly characteristic of Beethoven. The latter had provided his Ninth Symphony, for Schott in Mayence, with metronome-marks; Ries, too, had requested them for London. But the first copy had been lost, time was pressing, and Beethoven "was, therefore, obliged to go through with this unpleasant procedure for a second time." The task was hardly completed, when Schindler found the earlier copy; and behold, "a comparison showed a deviation of the tempo in every movement. Thereupon the master exclaimed angrily: ' No metronome at all ! Whoever has the right feeling, needs none; and whoever lacks it, has no use for one—he will run away with the whole orchestra anyhow.' " — Later, nevertheless, he again had recourse to the metronome !

It is greatly to be desired, in order to render the metronome an instrument of real utility,* that composers should regard any given tempo-mark as expressing an established tempo indicated, within certain fixed limits, by metronomic figures; a habit to which one could readily become accustomed. We therefore take the liberty of offering, with due deference, the following proposition :

Among the regularly recurring sounds of nature, those caused by human footsteps appear specially adapted for a foundation-tempo. In fact, certain expressions in music (*e.g.*, the German "gehen," to go, walk, and the Italian "andante," going, walking) point directly to this idea. The metronome-scale is based on divisions of the minute (*e.g.*, $\quad = 120$ means 120 beats to the minute); on trying to keep step with these beats we find that 120 steps to the minute conform to an energetic, manly, but by no means hasty walking-pace. This tempo might well be described as " Allegro alla marcia," or " Allegro moderato." We should, of course, allow a deviation of ten degrees above and below (110-130) for the modifications of such a simple Allegro, from Allegro maestoso to Allegro risoluto, etc. Our figure 120 is, perhaps, too low for an average Allegro,† but is convenient to

* It is positively indispensable as an arbitrator of disputes between executants.
† The average for an ordinary concert Allegro might be set at about 132.

remember, being twice the number of seconds in a minute; and we can, if necessary, fix our tempi according to a watch. By halving this 120, we obtain ♪ = 60, or 60 steps per minute (1 per second), the walking-pace of a person lost in thought, or creeping away in sorrow. This tempo we term Adagio. Twenty degrees higher, ♩ = 80, is the gait of an easy promenade, which perhaps best corresponds to the idea of Andante. Twenty degrees higher still, ♩ = 100, carry us toward the brisker motion of the Allegretto. In like manner, 20 degrees above the simple Allegro would give ♩ = 140, Allegro con brio or vivace; ♩ = 160 would represent Allegro molto; and, finally, Presto would be ♩ = 180. These quarter-notes, in slow $\frac{2}{4}$ time, for instance, would have to be changed to eighth-notes.* We shall not deny that a more rational system for fixing the tempo might be devised; the following general view of the proposed system of metronomic marking will render it easier to form an opinion on its value :

	BEATS.
Adagio	= 60 (50–70)
Andante	= 80 (70–90)
Allegretto	= 100 (90–110)
Allegro (moderato)	= 120 (110–130)
Allegro con brio (vivace)	= 140 (130–150)
Allegro molto	= 160 (150–170)
Presto	= 180.—

Adagio : Allegro mod. : : 1 : 2
Allegro mod. : Presto : : 2 : 3
Adagio : Presto : : 1 : 3.

An interesting remark of Beethoven's on the meaning of the term "Andantino" has been transmitted to us through his correspondence

---

* Considerable modifications are likewise to be noted (at least according to Czerny's metronome-marks in the " Kunst des Vortrags ") even on account of the division of the measure into two, three, or four parts ; for the Allegro movements in ¢ and $\frac{2}{4}$ time are, on an average, slower, those in $\frac{3}{4}$ time faster, than those in C time, counting by beats in the case of the former, and by quarter-notes in the case of the latter.

with Thomson. He begs the latter, " wherever a song (to be arranged)
is marked Andantino, to inform him whether it should be slower or faster
than Andante ; for the signification of this word, like so many others in
music, is so uncertain, that Andantino sometimes approaches Allegro,
and is sometimes played like Adagio." [Thayer, III, 241.] Even now,
views are still at variance on this point.

.   .   .   .   .   .

An important sub-head in the question of tempo in Beethoven's
piano-works is

**The rate of speed at which single beats, measures, or
passages are to be taken within a given tempo-mark.**

Hardly any theory appears at first glance so seductive, and probably
no other can count so many partisans, as the doctrine of *free interpretation*, or (as far as it applies here) the doctrine of freedom in time in
the artistic interpretation of Beethoven's compositions ; it is, indeed, at-
tested and preached by a man who was intimate, as a pupil and friend,
with Beethoven in his later years—Anton Schindler.

In substantiation of his views, Schindler formulates one of his teacher's precepts as follows :

" ' Although a poet writes his monologue or dialogue in a regular,
progressive rhythm, the reciter must, none the less, observe certain
divisions and pauses in order to bring out the sense, even where the
poet could not indicate them by punctuation ; and this style of declamation is equally applicable to music, and is modified only by the
number of participants in the execution of the given work.' " (Biography, 3rd ed., p. 213.)

Enlarging upon free interpretation (p. 225), Schindler remarks that
it may rightly be asserted that " at the present time [the Preface to the
3rd ed. is dated 1858] the true conception of *free interpretation* is
utterly lost." He then goes on to deny the identity of the conceptions
free interpretation and *tempo rubato* with reference to the " earlier
(classic) art-epoch." " It must be observed, at the outset, that the

term *free interpretation* was wrongly held to mean the same thing as the *tempo rubato* of the Italian singer. The mere fact that the latter term is employed chiefly in *opera buffa*, while hardly known in *opera seria*, shows that such a conception is at least indefinite. Beethoven protested against the use of this term in his music." * And now he ridicules Seyfried's statement, according to which Beethoven, when conducting, insisted "on great precision" with regard to an "effective *tempo rubato*," remarking thereon: "A *tempo rubato* even in orchestral music!" Further on he gives a few æsthetic quotations (not all of which, however, refer to rhythmic freedom), and finally culminates with the sentence: "The author must emphatically avouch, that whatever he heard performed by Beethoven corresponded wholly (with few exceptions) to the foregoing precepts; it was free from any constraint in time, precisely as the spirit of the composition might require. . . ."

For the clearer elucidation of Schindler's theory, we add several of his examples of "Beethoven's rhetoric"; "the cæsura which he often employed, and the rhetorical pause, both derived from Clementi" [N. B.!], likewise of "the points of repose, where they are not explicitly marked by the composer."

In the C-minor Sonata, op. 10, "from measure 13 to 21 inclusive, we find the rhetorical pause"; an example follows the description:

"All the written quarter-rests in the higher part are to be aug-

* We do not know what the buffo singers of the period understood by "*tempo rubato*." There is no doubt that Ph. E. Bach and Türk took it to mean something quite different from an alteration between *accel.* and *ritard.* Türk writes (Chap. VI, Sect. 5, § 72): "That is, there is taken (stolen) from one note something of its time-value, and more given therefor to another note; *e.g.*

Hence we perceive, that in this style of playing the *tempo*, or rather the *time*, is not deranged as a whole."

mented by about two, the interrupted phrase being thrown off with vehemence. The aim is, to increase the suspense."

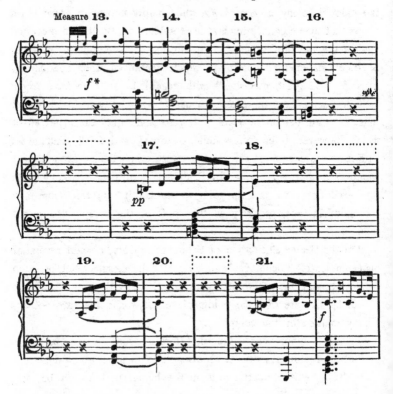

"The Cadenza before the Coda in the first division of this movement . . . shows the application of the Beethoven precept; that is, points of repose, *where they are not explicitly marked by the composer*. These are intended, besides, to mark the dividing-line of the Coda."

* As to the *"f"* in this phrase "to be thrown off with vehemence," it is possible that Schindler made a slight error. An edition by Breitkopf & Härtel which we have at hand, likewise that by Simrock-Czerny, has here only *rinf.* (or *rfz.*). (Only *"p"* precedes.) An old Haslinger edition, Section I, No. 8, "by permission of Bermann," has *rinf.* two measures before, and no sign at all here. An earlier Br. & H. edition, No. 7837, repeats the Haslinger *rinf.* two measures later.

Touching the Largo of the D-major Sonata, op. 10, Schindler quotes from Czerny's "Kunst des Vortrags": "'In this Largo, too, a well-calculated *ritardando* and *accelerando* must enhance the effect. Thus, for example, the second half only [this "only" is Schindler's interpolation] of the 23rd measure should be played somewhat faster; similarly the second half of measures 27 and 28. In like manner, from measure 71 to 75, there should be an intensification in animation and power, with a return to the former tranquillity in measure 76.'"

But all this is not enough for Schindler. "For the interpretation of this pregnant movement, according to Beethoven, *wellnigh ten several changes in the rate of motion* [*ergo*, actual change of tempo !?] are requisite, mostly perceptible only to a delicate ear." [N. B. !]

In the year 1814 Schindler, "as a poor student," made Beethoven's personal acquaintance ["Biography," 3rd ed., I, 229 *et seq.*; also Thayer, III, 277–8], this being the very time at which Beethoven bade farewell to the public, as a player, in the repeated performance of his B♭-major Trio, op. 97. [Th., III, 278.] Schindler was then but eighteen. His chief period of study under Beethoven was probably during the years 1818 to 1821 ["Biogr.," I, 14, and II, 231]. Fortunately, however, our attention has been called, through a quotation by Nottebohm, to the circumstance that Schindler, in the first edition of his Biography (publ. 1840), made another important observation on the

---

* The bracketted [*ff*] and [*sfz.*] (or *rfz.*), together with the slur indicated by dots, were omitted by Schindler. The slur is in the above-mentioned editions. (In the parallel passage at the close of the second division, the Haslinger edition gives only the beginning of the slur at the second beat.)

matter in hand.   It reads as follows [p. 228.—Nottebohm, " Metronom.
Bezeichnungen," p. 134, Note.   (Slightly abbreviated.)] : "What I
myself heard Beethoven play *was always, with few exceptions, free of
all restraint in tempo;* a 'tempo rubato' in the most exact meaning
of the term, as required by the conception and conditions, but without
even the slightest trace of a caricature. *

"It was the most distinct and intelligible declamation," etc. . . .
" His older friends, who had attentively followed the development of his
mind in every direction, affirmed that he did not assume this manner
of performance until the first years of his third period, then having
quite forsaken his earlier, less expressively varied, manner." (In this
same first edition he goes on to say : "Several of the sonatas, however,

* In this same edition Schindler says, touching Beethoven's performance of
the E-major Sonata, op. 14 (Allegro, $\mathbf{C}$) : " With the entrance of the middle
movement

the dialogue became sentimental, and the ruling tempo Andante [N. B.], yet very
vacillating, for at the entrance of each repetition of the theme a brief pause was
made on the first note, about like this :

," etc.

" The second movement (Allegretto) was, as played by Beethoven, more like
an Allegro furioso [N. B. !], and, excepting the single chord

on which he delayed very long, he retained the same tempo.—In the Maggiore
the tempo was more moderate . . . " [N. B. !]—Then tempo-marks are mean-
ingless !

are to be played strictly in time, properly admitting of but a few deviations, or none at all, and still less demanding them. Such are those
which require bravura in their execution, for instance op. 106 [comp.
about 1818], op. 111 [about 1822 : Nottebohm], besides op. 57 [be-
longing to the second period], and some others!")

Now, the third period began, according to Schindler, about the
year 1815 ; and among Beethoven's older friends was Ries, who assured
us that Beethoven **"usually kept strict time "** ; and consequently,
as far as our Concertos are concerned, we have nothing more to add.
For, even supposing that Beethoven ever performed them later (in
private), and then played them in his changed manner, our primary
intention was to reconstruct our ideal as nearly as possible in resem-
blance to the composer's conception at the time when he wrote
them ; and it would be difficult to assume that Beethoven *conceived*
his concertos (or at least the first four) as *free* in tempo, and nevertheless *played* them in *strict* tempo. It would be equally difficult to
assume (*cf.* page 17) that Beethoven did not gain a *truer*, or *the true*,
conception of the concertos which he had composed in the preceding
periods, as well as of the majority of his works for pianoforte, until his
third period. Ries, to be sure, also notes exceptions, one of which we
utilized for the close of the Fourth Concerto ; and Czerny specifies
further deviations from the ruling tempo in the last three concertos
("Kunst des Vortrags)" [we shall not enter into details] ; but, after
what has been said above, *the idea of regular rhythmic freedom
must be dismissed.*

It is true that the freedom of delivery "is modified* by the number
of participants in the execution of the given work " ; and in piano-concertos one should assume, at the outset, strictness of rhythm as a necessary condition. There is, however, a peculiar kind of rhythmic freedom, which consists in the moderation of the tempo throughout entire
passages, and which, in the case of piano-concertos, is not merely
possible, but is expressly sanctioned by Schindler ; though it cannot
be positively affirmed that this sanction includes the Beethoven Con-

* See page 24.

certos: "It may be said in general, concerning the free delivery of piano-music in the period behind us, that it was chiefly limited to a changed, moderated tempo in the *cantabile* passages of the Allegro movements, almost regularly recurring in the episodes and coda. [N. B.] In this respect, Hummel's remarks on the changes of tempo in the *cantilenas* of his Grand Concerto in A minor may be regarded as classic examples." [3rd ed., II, 230.]

On examining Hummel's Pianoforte-Method, we found, for the first Solo of the A-minor Concerto, some seven different directions for the tempo. For instance, at the entrance of the Solo, "From here onward, moderate in tempo"; then, at the passage in sixteenth-notes, "From here somewhat livelier and more marked"; at the theme in C major, "The middle division somewhat *ritenuto*, and with feeling"; eight measures further on, "Faster, and with animation"; etc., etc. But in the Note Hummel adds: "All yieldingness in single measures, at short, singing passages or pleasing episodical ideas, must be scarcely perceptible, and not be dragged into an *adagio;* the difference between the *ritenuto* and the *accelerando* must never form too marked a contrast with the principal tempo. . . ."

There is no occasion for our disputing with Hummel over these "scarcely perceptible" rhythmic changes, which he liked in his own works. Whether Beethoven, in his first and second periods, subscribed to such views, would appear all the more questionable from Schindler's own remarks: "True, even in the new style of piano-playing inaugurated by Hummel, the aim was to do full justice to the *cantilena*, for the most part in accordance with the Italian method of singing. . . ."

For our own part, we can imagine a very beautiful delivery of the second theme in Beethoven's C-minor Concerto, for instance,

without necessitating a moderation of the principal tempo, presupposing that this principal tempo were not taken too fast from the beginning.

For the rest, that we, and probably Ries, too, understand by "strictness in tempo" only the strictness of a steady musician, and not an invariable and absolute coincidence with the strokes of a metronome, hardly needs to be added. We are also well aware that even the steadiest musician warms to his work, and calms down at a fitting opportunity; and it may be said, in general, that occasional slight *ritardandi* at transitional passages, on the resumption of the main theme, or before *fermate*, are most to be recommended among all subjective deviations from the tempo, and may be employed in concertos, in so far as they are applicable, in unaccompanied passages.

Finally, there are passages in remote keys in which the composer's spirit appears to roam in far distant regions, and in which an imperceptible vacillation or yielding in the tempo seems to present itself to the impressionable executant; *e.g.*, in the G-major Concerto, page 6 of our edition:

But these are *nuances* which should neither be sought nor strongly marked, and should rarely be employed.

It is *possible* that Beethoven, in his Third Period, whose stylistic peculiarities we apparently recognize in works as early as op. 78 and 81 (Les Adieux; comp. 1809), acquired greater rhythmic freedom of delivery. Traces of this freedom might be found in the somewhat more frequent use of short *ritardandi* and *accelerandi;* further, it may happen that where a musical idea ends at a bar—a peculiarity of the later works—and the new idea begins directly thereafter, the interpolation of a short pause between the two becomes necessary; still, we doubt the advisability of increasing the number of deviations in tempo which are indicated in the works themselves, by others which are in the least degree striking. (For example, one might be inclined to take the beginning of op. 101 somewhat *rubato;* but in the fifth measure, a "*poco ritard.*" by the composer shows us that the previous one ought to be only *pochissimo*. Further on, "*espressivo e semplice*" also warns against overstepping proper limits.) But to apply a style of delivery, applicable to the works of this period, directly to the earlier compositions, would indeed be like pouring new wine into old bottles. And to specify two rates of speed for the principal theme and the episodes, and to reckon, metronome in hand, differences of ten degrees or more for an Allegro of the Second Period—this strikes us as not simply imperilling unity of tempo, but as opening the floodgates to [arbitrary] rhythmical effects.

Again, it is possible that Beethoven, who, more especially in later years, appears to have indulged in various rhythmic speculations—(he planned, as Schindler [3rd ed., II, p. 183] narrates, " to write a Piano-forte-Method himself," which he intended to be " something quite out of the common ")—himself experimented, in this respect, with his earlier works; we should likewise find it very natural, had he mistakenly applied the knowledge acquired through his metrical studies, necessitated by his vocal compositions [*cf.* Thayer, II, p. 88], to the performance of his piano-works. It is also possible, that the " Klimpern " [jingling] of young Schindler, whom he pushed away from the piano with a not exactly flattering remark ["Biogr.," I, 14, and II, 231], vexed him, and that he consequently exaggerated, which may easily happen to other teachers; and finally, it is possible that Schindler often thought he heard things which were not at all in the music.

·   ·   ·   ·   ·   ·

More important than his theory of rhythmic freedom, are Schindler's statements concerning Beethoven's dynamic means of expression. The agency for their manifestation is the Touch. We are told, on page 231, that Beethoven retained a "forceful" and "virile" touch until the close of his life. What Schindler has to say further on [3rd ed., II, 237] about the touch and its "dual significance—the physical or material, and the psychical," "to which Clementi * had drawn attention," and "which Beethoven considered highly important," strikes us, again, as belonging rather to the domain of theoretical speculation. On the other hand, the following statement is well worthy of notice: "Altogether, our Master was a declared opponent of miniature-painting in musical interpretation of all kinds, and, therefore, demanded forcible expression everywhere. The performances of the Schuppanzigh Quartet were a further proof of this. In *forte* these four men brought out the effect of a small orchestra, in total contrast to the languid, sickly-sweet, affected style of very celebrated quartets of our day" (*i.e.*, before 1858). Of course, neither Schindler nor the editor wishes it to be understood that delicate passages should not be delicately played; for the rest, Schindler's meaning is too clear to require further commentary.

"In the *cantilena* he [Beethoven] pointed to the method of educated singers, who do not go to extremes; he also advised the writing of suitable words under disputed passages, and then singing them, or to hear such passages played by a trained violinist or player on some wind-instrument."

---

* "He [Clementi] understood as appertaining to this latter class the fullness of tone anticipated by the feeling before the finger touches the key. One who has not experienced this, will never soulfully perform an Adagio."—But then he will be unable to bring out any dynamic *nuances* whatever! Our fingers ought to be so schooled by practice as to carry out instinctively and without more ado each and every dynamic intention.

Beethoven's Piano Playing

An essential feature in the singing of "educated singers" is the well-calculated swell and subsidence of one or more tones. The latter *nuance* is also practicable on the pianoforte. However strongly we are opposed, in general, to arbitrary changes of tempo in our Concertos, we still feel obliged to declare that even with an exact observance of all dynamic expression-marks a "soulful" interpretation is not arrived at. As long as nothing more is done, the interpretation will usually prove stiff and void of expression; and the hearer may well say, "The performance did not move me." Quite on the contrary, it will happen comparatively seldom in a warmly emotional interpretation, that the notes of long or even of short phrases follow each other with exactly the same degree of force. In a *cantilena*, more particularly, hardly any two or three successive notes will be played with equal strength. Were the composer to mark all these places, he would have to cover almost every page with < and >, and in polyphonic passages several such signs might occur in one measure! Our classic composers, and Beethoven himself in his first three Concertos, were very chary in the use of expression-marks. They left the slighter *nuances* to the feeling of the player, indicating only the most prominent lines. Hence, as a matter of course, these subjective *nuances* of expression must give precedence to those prescribed by the composer. We must also observe that, just as the graduated transition from one contrast to another, by swelling or subsiding, is frequently a beauty, an abrupt juxtaposition of contrasts may, under certain conditions, produce the better effect. Beethoven is fond of letting a *piano* passage follow after a *crescendo*. Indeed, it is sometimes not easy to determine where one of his crescendos should cease. For instance, in the theme of the A♭-major Sonata, op. 26, it seems to us improbable that the *cresc.* here

should continue through the entire two measures; and again, in this same theme, a *sf* appears to mark the climax,

as the *cresc.* is soon repeated.—Beethoven employed the dashes of prolongation after *cresc.*, = = = =, or according to Nottebohm ["Beethoveniana," XXIV.], *cresc.* — – — —, from about the year 1806. In our Concertos we find them for the first time in the Fourth (publ. 1808) in a few places, and here in the form "cres — — cen — — do"; also in the autograph of the E♭ Concerto as "cres. = = = " (the earliest edition known to us, by Br. & H., No. 1613, has only rarely "cresc. — — —"; a later one, with precisely the same title and No., corrects these slips). In such cases the dashes of prolongation very practically indicate the continuance of the effect, and also serve as a reminder that it should be suitably graduated.

A feature which seems to have lent peculiar charm to Beethoven's playing, and one which we, too, reckon among the chief requisites of a fine interpretation, was the Accentuation.

"It was, more especially, the *rhythmical* accent which he generally desired to have strongly brought out," says Schindler [3rd ed., II, 236]; "on the other hand, he usually treated the melodical (generally termed the grammatical [?]) accent as the situation required [!], only being in the habit of accenting all suspensions, particularly that of the minor second in *cantabile*, more emphatically than other players whom we had heard. This imbued his playing with a characteristic pregnancy quite different from the smooth, shallow performances which never reach the height of tone-speech." We owe Schindler special gratitude for these observations.

True, for consistency's sake [*cf.* page 8], we ought to ask: "What part, or how much, of these remarks by S. is applicable to Beethoven's Third Period?"—However, aside from the fact that with reference to this feature we have no direct counterstatements to record, it is likely that the above-mentioned shadings were too closely knit with Beethoven's character and individuality not to claim a certain general validity for all periods of his life.

"All appoggiaturas are to be struck more forcibly than the following note," was already said by Ph. E. Bach ["Essay," 3rd ed., Chap. II, § 7], who also remarks: "However, one can observe that Dissonances are generally played stronger and Consonances weaker, because the former emphatically fire the passions and the latter soothe them." [Essay, Chap. III, "On Interpretation," § 29; the entire chapter is both interesting and instructive.] A composer of such deep and fiery feeling as Beethoven had no need of reading such sentences beforehand, in order to make the above-described pregnant rhythms his own. The fact of his usually accenting the suspension of the minor second more strongly than "other players," would indicate that this was not the effect of mere speculation, of a Clementi tradition, but that it sprang from a wholly original mental [temperamental] disposition. And finally, concerning the delivery of the *cantilena*, he had had (supposing him to need a pattern) in early youth, in the theatre, vocal examples (even if not invariably classic ones), and as early as 1791 was himself, according to the judgment of Chaplain Junker, "as good a player in Adagio as Allegro." In view of all these attributes, only the degree of development would come in question; and so, in point of fact, we may well assume that the earlier works, of course with due consideration of their conception and character, are, on the whole, to be more simply interpreted than the later ones, yet without denying the former vital warmth of expression. In this case, to be sure, as in all artistic directions, genuine artistic talent is requisite to hit the golden mean.

In the foregoing observations we have dealt with so-called "tradition." There still remains, however, another resource of musical interpretation to be mentioned, which has latterly been placed well in the foreground, and has, indeed, developed quite new and peculiar ideas in theoretical instruction. We mean

The Art of Phrasing.

The idea is rather old; for Türk says, in his Pianoforte-Method * :
" Just as the words *Er verlor das Leben nicht nur sein Vermögen,* etc.
[He lost his life, not only his property] bear a wholly different sense according as a comma is set after *nicht* [not] or *Leben* [life], precisely so indistinct, or rather wrong, does the delivery of a musical idea become through incorrect punctuation." To indicate the punctuation, he employs the sign //, *e.g.,*

Now-a-days, the comma, borrowed from written language, is often used; and in instructive editions its utility is unquestioned, as it admonishes the pupil to take his finger from the key (the "lift"). But music has its own signs of punctuation, such as rests,† holds, staccato-marks, and slurs. At the rests and staccatos, and likewise at the holds (*fermate*), the lifting of the finger is a matter of course; it is only the slurs that often vex both player and editor. As may be seen from the example in the footnote, and from that next following, one cannot always identify the end of a slur in Beethoven with a "lift," or musical comma. The beginning of the second theme in the C-minor Concerto, according to the Original Edition published " A Vienne au Bureau

* "Clavierschule," 1789; Chap. VI, Sec. 2: "On Musical Punctuation."
He does not remember having read anything on this head in any method of piano-playing, and, therefore, appears to claim priority of invention.

† For instance, in Beethoven's Second Concerto :

d'Arts et d'Industrie," No. 289, and also in our own, is marked for the first time with the following slurs:

But no one would actually care to separate the first two measures from each other. Even if no slurs at all were given, only one bad mistake in phrasing would be possible in the first eight measures; namely, if one should play like this:

but such a player would be somewhat unmusical. At the repetition in C major, indeed, the slurring is thus:

This may be a mere slip; or perhaps the composer did not intend a separation after the dotted quarter-note (further on we shall meet with a similar case); in any event, it is clear that in Beethoven the slurs are to be regarded in only a very general sense as legato-signs. Only in very short figures of two or three notes, *e.g.*, in the B♭-major Concerto, Adagio:

would there appear to be an express direction for lifting the finger.

Where the musical training is good, we think there is little serious danger of insufficient or incorrect phrasing; the danger seems to us to lie rather in overloading the phrasing, as a direct consequence of modern efforts. The mistake may, perhaps, be found in the endeavor to transfer certain peculiarities of some other instrument, *e.g.*, the bowing of the violin, to piano-technique.

Even the celebrated author of a work on Greek metrics has quite recently attempted to apply the laws of ancient metre (more especially of song) to modern piano-music. This highly interesting work is entitled: "A General Theory of Musical Rhythmics since Johann Sebastian Bach, founded on the Ancient, etc.," by Rudolph Westphal.* We shall give merely a few examples applicable to Beethoven's work, with some preliminary elucidations.

The smallest time-unit in Music, Language, and the Dance was called, by the Greeks, *chronos protos* (◡ 𝅘𝅥𝅯, or 𝅘𝅥𝅮, or 𝅘𝅥). Two chronoi protoi form, combined, one "long syllable" in prosody (◡ ◡ = –; 𝅘𝅥𝅯 𝅘𝅥𝅯 = 𝅘𝅥𝅮; 𝅘𝅥𝅮 𝅘𝅥𝅮 = 𝅘𝅥, etc.). A prosodic foot (or musical measure) is formed by combining long and short syllables (– ◡ ◡, – ◡; 𝅘𝅥𝅮 𝅘𝅥𝅮 𝅘𝅥𝅯, 𝅘𝅥𝅮 𝅘𝅥𝅯, etc.). There are three principal species of feet or "measures": the Dactyl (– ◡ ◡); the Iambus (◡ –), and the Pæan (– ◡ ◡ ◡). From the simplest "measures," compound measures are formed. These latter can, however, attain to only a fixed maximum of extension, which is calculated according to the number of "time-units" (*chronoi protoi*) contained therein; thus, dactylic measure may contain not more than 16, iambic only 18, and pæanic only 25 such time-units. Longer combinations would overpass our sense for rhythmic unity.†

* The German title is: "Allgemeine Theorie der musikalischen Rhythmik seit Joh. Seb. Bach." Publ. 1880, by Breitkopf & Härtel, Leipzig.

† "Griechische Metrik," 2d ed., I, p. 542 *et seq.;* II, p. 126 *et seq.* *E.g.*, where the least time-unit is a 16th-note, as in the first C-minor Fugue in the "Well-tempered Clavichord," the longest *kolon* cannot be extended, according to the Greek idea, beyond the scope of a four-four measure, which need not, however, be bounded by the bars, but should be divided (in this case) as follows:

(Quoted in "Mus. Rhythmik," pp. 64, 111, 113, 114, 188, 201; completely analyzed on p. 268.) This conclusion of Aristoxenes' observations closely conforms to modern musical theory, so that we can apply Aristoxenes' rules to our music, with the sole exception that in our music indisputable examples of dactylic kola having six feet are to be found." (Ibid., p. 100.)

By combining such *kola* (members) we first obtain the Period (series; Lat. *versus*), and, by combining periods, the Strophe. Within any given species of measure, however, the several *kola* must contain a fixed number of actual *chronoi protoi; e.g.*, in the dactylic, 4, 8, 12, or 16; otherwise they are completed by pauses or rests (*leimmata*), or by means of extension (prolongation, tone). At the termination of each *kolon* comes a *cæsura*, which, in spoken language, is usually coincident with the end of a word (in Greek the cæsura need not occur till the end of a period).

Now, in modern music, the termination of a *kolon* should also be indicated to the ear by a cæsura, *e.g.*, by interrupting the legato.*

It seems to us, however, that our author either overlooked, or gave too slight consideration to the fact, that the ancient metricians, in settling the limits of the *kola* and periods, had to be guided not merely by the necessities of rhythmic unity, but were obliged, above all, to reckon with the imperative exigencies of taking breath (in greater or less quantity). But such an exigency does not exist for the pianist's fingers, at least. We have compositions in which slurs pass over uninterrupted series of 16th-notes from bar to bar, or from line to line, and might be extended equally well over entire pages. The cæsura ("lift") is excluded: *kolon* follows *kolon* in an unbroken chain. But Professor Westphal likewise finds fault with the slurring in the *cantilena* passages of Beethoven's works in the Moscheles and other editions; he requires, for instance (p. 150), for the second movement of the *Sonate pathétique*, the following phrasing:

* "We define the musical *kolon* as a group of several feet belonging to the same rhythmic species. Such a group is held together, as a rhythmic unit, by elevating one of the accents of the combined feet to the principal accent in the *kolon*, and by dividing the *kolon* from the neighboring *kola* by a perceptible marking of the boundary-line" (p. 92). The boundary-line of the *kolon* is designated as a cæsura on p. 93; and the half-*kolon* ("Binnen-Cäsur") is also mentioned there. The Cæsura is treated in detail on p. 106 *et seq.*—On pp. 93 and (particularly) 107, he says that the tones belonging to one *kolon* are "executed legato,

But by referring to the following three editions: that of Breitkopf & Härtel, No. 11,461, of Steingräber, and of Czerny-Simrock, we find that their slurring agrees with that in the Moscheles edition:

and although we have not asserted that the hand *ought to be lifted at the end* of every slur, the opposite conclusion is not justifiable, that the hand *may* be lifted *under* a slur. That could be justified only by very peculiar conditions, like the assumption of an engraver's mistake. Perhaps the composer wished, in this very place, to prevent a "lift"?

Another example. According to Professor Westphal (pp. 117 *et seq.*), the first theme of the A♭-major Sonata, op. 26, in "Ionic rhythm," should be executed thus:

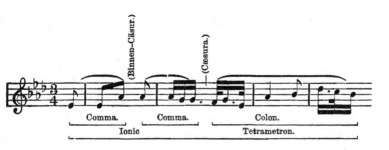

In this case we are happily able to assure our readers that, according to the composer's Autograph [in the Royal Library, Berlin], and also according to an edition in oblong form by Cappi, the original publisher,*

unless rests occur"; the "interruption of the legato" takes place only at the cæsura.—On p. 113 he finds fault with the staccato, saying that it ought to be limited to comic or highly tragic effects in instrumental music.

* "Grande Sonate . . .", etc., corresponding with the title given by Nottebohm for the earliest edition (advertised in 1802), "par Lovis van Beethoven / Œuvre 26. / À Vienne chez Jean Cappi / Sur la Place St. Michel No. 4." Register 880. Price 2 fl. Nottebohm has "Louis" for *Lovis*, "à" (small), and added punctuation-marks; address and price are omitted. (Thayer's Chronol. Cat. has the same address.) In this edition we also find the bars scored through. Possibly only the title belongs to the first edition in this form.

the passage in question is marked as follows with regard to the *legato* and *staccato* :

The above-mentioned more modern editions also accept this slurring.

III

ON THE TRILL

Although we also consider the correct execution of a trill to be one of the requirements of a fine delivery, we devote a separate chapter to the discussion of this matter; first, because we cannot give our readers much positive information regarding Beethoven, and, secondly, because a review of the question compels us to begin at a considerably earlier date. We shall not deal, of course, with æsthetic directions touching evenness, rapidity, and the like, but rather with a point more or less in dispute in other cases as well, namely,

Shall the trill begin on principal tone or auxiliary ?

Now, in accord with the great majority of the hints and teachings of German and French composers and theorists of the eighteenth century,

The ordinary trill should begin on the higher auxiliary, which may, however, be written in the form of a long appoggiatura.

Real or apparent deviations from this fundamental rule will be noted later, while discussing the several musicians.

To elucidate the reason for this phenomenon, it might be of utility to trace back the theory of appoggiaturas to its beginning. However, as we have to do with facts only, we may be satisfied with the exact explanation given by Marpurg concerning the Development of the Trill out of the Appoggiatura.[*]

"The Trill originated in the conjunct appoggiatura from above downward, and is, fundamentally, nothing more than a series of appoggiaturas following each other with the greatest rapidity. The usual

[*] Marpurg, "Anleitung zum Clavierspielen," 1st ed., Berlin, 1755; Chap. I, Sec. 9, "On the Trill," § 1.

definition, which describes it as the swift alternation of a tone with the second above, does not conflict with this new explanation."

The further development of the trill is described by Ph. E. Bach. *

"Before this they [trills] were not lightly employed, except after an appoggiatura or on the repetition of the preceding note; in the former case they are termed "angeschlossene Triller" (conjunct trills); but nowadays they occur after leaping notes, directly at the beginning, often one after the other, at Cadenzas, over long *fermate*, at the ends of divisions, *without* a preceding appoggiatura, and also *after* one. Consequently, this grace is much more arbitrary now than formerly."

We learn where the proper and regular place for the trill was from Tosi's "Anleitung zur Singkunst," translated and provided with explanations by Agricola, Royal Prussian Court Composer. [Berlin, 1757.] "Any one who can execute a really fine trill, has the advantage of being able to finish the cadences or closes of a song creditably, the place where the trill is most decidedly essential." [Tosi.]

Probably because of this association with the cadences, the trill was called "cadence" (besides "tremblement") in France.

On this head J. J. Rousseau's "Dictionnaire de Musique" says: "As a term in singing, *cadence* means the beating in the throat which the Italians call *trillo*, which we otherwise call *tremblement*, and which is usually made on the penultimate note of a musical phrase; whence it doubtless took the name of Cadence."

Having thus sufficiently informed ourselves concerning the origin and regular place of the trill, we give in chronological order the most important directions for its

Execution.

Couperin, surnamed *le Grand* [1668–1733], gives in his "Pièces de Clavecin" [1713] the following "explication" of the trill. [Plate and Explanation of the Embellishments.]

* "Essay on the True Method of Playing the Pianoforte"; 1st ed., 1753; 3d ed., 1787. Chap. III, "On Trills," § 1.

NOTE. "⌐⎯⎯⎯⎤ is a sign to mark notes which should be bound and slurred."

In "L'art de toucher le clavecin" [1717], Couperin adds the following explanation:

"Trills of any considerable extent comprise three parts, which coalesce to one in execution: (1) The suspension, which should be formed on the note above the principal note; (2) The trill-beats; and (3) the final tone * (point of repose).

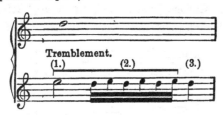

"As to the other trills, they are arbitrary. Some have the suspen-

* *Cf.* Marpurg's trill-terminations, further on.

sion; others are so short as to have neither suspension nor point of repose."

To present this theory in full, we add J. J. Rousseau's explanation ("Dict. de Musique") from the second half of the eighteenth century: "There are two kinds of Cadences; one is the *Cadence pleine*, and consists in not beginning the beating of the voice until the higher note has been dwelt on; the other is called *Cadence brisée*, and in it the beatings begin quite without preparation:"

[EDITOR'S NOTE. The + is an early sign for *tr*. In the execution of the first example, we find a case of the abbreviation of a short note after a dot.]

Could Seb. Bach have read these "explications" of Couperin's? —In a copy, prepared by Fuchs, of a copy made by Bach of two French suites [by Grigny and Dieupart; R. Library, Berlin], occur the following examples of trills:

Tremblement simple.   Tremblement appuyé.

Bach himself, in the *"Clavierbüchlein* for Wilhelm Friedemann Bach, begun at Cöthen, January 22d, A.D. 1720," left the following definition of the trill (here transferred from the C-clef to the violin-clef):

Trillo.

For his part, he calls the *turn* a " Cadence " :

The suspension (appoggiatura) he calls the " Accent " (rising and fall-

ing) :

steigend.   fallend.

" Accent and Trillo : "

Execution :

J. S. Bach's colleague at Weimar, court musician and organist Johann Gottfried Walther, a celebrated teacher, writes in his Lexicon [1732] : " **Trillo,** pl. *trilli* (Ital.) is a grace in singing and playing, for the execution of which, according to situation or signature, either the major or minor second is employed, this note being struck, in alternation with the note written on the paper, and marked with *tr* or *t*, rapidly and distinctly, beginning on the higher note and ending on the lower (*i.e.*, the written or principal note)." Here we have a very categorical explanation, not to be misunderstood, on the beginning and end of the trill.

" **Trilletto,** pl. *trilletti* (Ital.), signifies that the trill is to be made short."—We shall return to this Trilletto.

The first work which we meet with in the second half of the eighteenth century, is Johann Joachim Quantz's " Versuch einer Anweisung die Flöte zu spielen." [Essay on the Method of Playing the Flute.]— The first edition, of 1752, appeared in French : " Essai d'une Méthode, etc., Berlin chez Ch. Fr. Voss." It still gives trills as " tremblemens." We quote from the third ed., Breslau, 1789 ; our quotations are found in both editions. Quantz still starts with the appoggiaturas (Chap. IX, § 7) :

" Every trill begins on the appoggiatura before its principal note, this appoggiatura being taken either from above or from below, as explained in the preceding chapter. . . ." 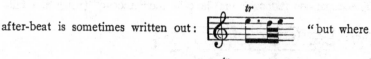 The

after-beat is sometimes written out: 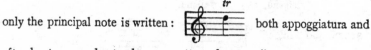 "but where

only the principal note is written:  both appoggiatura and

after-beat are understood as a matter of course."

§ 10 is also worthy of notice: "When the trill-sign stands over notes which form a dissonance with the fundamental part:

the appoggiatura before the trill must be very short, so as not to transform the dissonances into consonances."—Finally, we learn in Chap. VIII, § 14: "From the appoggiaturas some other small embellishments are derived; such as the Half-trill [der halbe Triller]:

 " etc.

The really leading theorist of Germany in the second half of the century was Carl Philipp Emanuel Bach, the son of Johann Sebastian. His famous "Essay on the True Method of Playing the Pianoforte" was first published in 1753. The directions given therein for the beginning of the ordinary trill, leave nothing to be desired on the score of simplicity and clearness. § 5 reads:

"The proper sign for the regular trill is ₩ (*a*); over long notes, this sign is lengthened (*b*). The trill always begins on the note above the (principal) tone; consequently, it is executed as at (*c*). It is superfluous to indicate it by a preceding grace-note (*d*), unless this grace-note is to be treated as an appoggiatura."

The more irregular does his "halber oder Pralltriller" [inverted mordent] appear (§ 30), which is distinguished from other trills by its

sharpness and shortness:

[EDITOR'S NOTE. We have added the dotted tie according to the description of the execution of this *Pralltriller*.]

It occurs "only before a falling second, to which it is slurred." With staccato notes, the "Schneller" serves as a substitute:

Two years after Bach's "Essay" came Marpurg with the first edition of his "Guide to Pianoforte-playing" [Anleitung zum Clavierspielen: 1755]. He assumes an independent position, which is peculiarly distinguished by the terminations of the trills. "Wherever a trill occurs, it must begin on the auxiliary note, and end on the principal note with a certain emphasis at the close, in order that, on ending, this principal note may be very distinctly felt."—His "compound or double trill" (zusammengesetzter oder Doppeltriller) has the following sign:

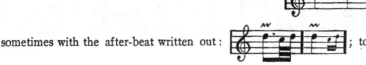

sometimes with the after-beat written out: ; to

be played .

For cases in which the auxiliary has just preceded the principal note on which the trill is made, Marpurg has a good and simple recipe: "When the auxiliary, on which the beat of a trill begins, directly precedes the principal note, this auxiliary is either repeated like a regular double appoggiatura [*Anschlag*], or, without repetition, bound to the following note like a suspension, before commencing the trill-beats:

The latter mode must be indicated by a slur."

In his conception of the *Pralltriller* [inverted mordent] Marpurg has freer views than his predecessors. "Whenever, in the conjunct simple trill, the conjunct auxiliary is passed over so that, contrary to rule, the trill begins directly on the principal tone, and the trill-beats are abbreviated and limited to only three notes, there will be formed a trill which, although incomplete, can nevertheless be better employed than the regular trill in certain cases. Such cases occur (*a*) in step-wise descending passages in a rapid tempo; likewise (*b*) when a short note is preceded by a long appoggiatura; or (*c*) when a note is abbreviated by an appoggiatura. . . . Herr Bach calls this trill a *Pralltriller* . . ."

One year after Marpurg follows Leopold Mozart with his "Thorough Violin-Method" (Gründliche Violinschule: 1756. The Preface is likewise printed in the second edition of 1770, from which we quote). According to his Preface, Mozart knew Marpurg, or, at least, the latter's "Kritische Beiträge." We do not know whether he had read Em. Bach's "Essay"; but he is acquainted with the *Pralltriller* under that name.—His first example (X, §2) of a trill is:

with him, too, it is the rule to begin on the auxiliary. In §5 he says: "Either beginning or end of a trill may be variously formed. The beats may commence directly from above,

or it [the trill] may be prepared by a descending appoggiatura, which is somewhat prolonged,

or by an ascending double appoggiatura with descent from the higher auxiliary,

or by the so-called Ribattuta:

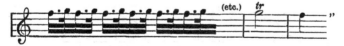

§ 11. "When a trill occurs in the midst of a passage, *e.g.*,

not only is an appoggiatura played before the trill, but this appoggiatura is held for half the time-value of the principal note:

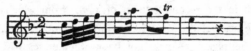

But when a passage begins with a trill, the appoggiatura is hardly heard, being then nothing but an emphatic leading-off of the trill; *e.g.,*

Finally, trills without appoggiatura also occur [§ 18]: "The first of four equal notes may be distinguished from the others by the trill without appoggiatura, by slurring the first two together in one bow, and then throwing off each of the other two with a separate bow; *e.g.,*

her. hin. her. hin. her. hin.

[*Heraufstrich*, or *her* = up-bow. *Hinunterstrich*, or *hin* = down-bow.]

Then, at the end of § 20, an example

her. hin. (etc.)

with the following explanation: "These trills, however, are only short and rapid trills without after-beat (*trilletti*) [Walther's trilletti?—see above], or so-called *Pralltriller*, which are not hard to learn for any one able to play a good ordinary trill. These short trills are as follows:

That is, they are *Pralltriller* of four notes, beginning on the higher auxiliary (which is not slurred), and thus essentially different from those described by Em. Bach.

Again, one year after the work last noticed, appeared the " Guide to the Art of Singing" (Anleitung zur Singkunst; publ. by Winter, Berlin, 1757), translated from the Italian of "Herrn Peter Franz Tosi" . . . with explanations and additions, by Johann Friedrich Agricola.

Tosi's opinion on the beginning of the trill is not quite plain.* But here we have to deal with Agricola. To the first, among eight different trills with which Tosi is acquainted (the ordinary trill with the major second†), Agricola appends the following example:

Agricola, therefore, begins on the auxiliary.—He knows Quantz and C. P. E. Bach.—His rules for the " half "-trill (" which may be recognized by its name alone" [Tosi]), are as follows : " Instrumentalists usually call this trill the *Pralltriller*. Pianists have adopted a special sign for it, namely, ～. It may be written thus in notes :

* Tosi wrote, according to Agricola's Preface, in 1723. Concerning appoggiaturas in general he says [Translation : p. 57] : " Now, if the pupil be sufficiently instructed in the matter, he will be so well acquainted with the appoggiaturas as to . . . be able to laugh at such composers as write out the appoggiaturas in notes." [!] This carries us back into a rather remote period.

† " The first is the greater trill, which is formed by the rapid alternation of two tones at an interval of a whole tone." (*a*) " One of these tones deserves the name of Principal Tone, because it has a right to fill out the place of the note which represents it, and is therefore, as it were, the master. The other tone, although situated in the next place above the former, is nothing more than the servant. From this trill are derived all other species of trill."—Does not this sound almost like a contradiction of Agricola's elucidation ?—On the other hand, Tosi says : " To render the trill fine, it should be prepared. But it does not invariably require an appoggiatura, for sometimes neither time nor good taste [!] would permit of one. But it demands the appoggiatura in almost all closing cadences, and in various places, now from the whole tone, and again from the semitone, above its principal note, as the key may require."—That sounds, in part, quite *modern !* But where are the places in which " good taste " omits the appoggiatura ?—Also *cf.* the French theories.

[That is, without a slur.] "When an appoggiatura precedes a *Pralltriller*, it forms the first note of the latter, which must not, therefore, be restruck. The case is different where the note, having the place of an appoggiatura, but written as a large note, is of brief time-value; *e.g.*,

Truly, a most subtle distinction! And how are we to understand the following comment by Agricola on the Closing Cadences mentioned here in the Note?—"Regular Trills . . . occur not only in cadences, and with appoggiaturas, but also quite free, and without the appoggiatura [do these begin on the principal note?] . . . and frequently even at the beginning of a piece."

After the analogy of his *Pralltriller*, in which the commencing higher auxiliary may in turn be bound to an appoggiatura, one might think that Agricola, diverging from French theory (or from Quantz), regards these appoggiaturas as independent tones, not to be identified with the beginning (?) auxiliary note of the trill. (Agricola was a pupil of J. S. Bach.)

With respect to the following theorists we can be briefer, satisfying ourselves mainly with examples. They derive more or less from their predecessors.

Löhlein's "Pianoforte-Method" (Clavierschule: 1st ed. 1765) knows Em: Bach and Marpurg.

In the year 1770, when the second edition of L. Mozart's Violin-Method appeared,

LUDWIG VAN BEETHOVEN

was born.

The next work in order is the " Guide to Musically Correct Singing " (Anweisung zum musikalisch richtigen Gesang; publ. by Junius at Leipzig, 1774), by the opera-composer Johann Adam Hiller, Cantor of the Thomasschule.—He knows Marpurg, Em. Bach, and Tosi-Agricola; the works of the two latter he considers to be " the best dissertations " on the embellishments.—According to Hiller (p. 38), the trill consists "of the frequent and rapid alternation of two tones . . . The lower is the principal tone, which supports the trill [*cf.* Tosi, above]; the higher tone however, has the right to begin." Examples:

That is, the first trill-note is slurred to the note preceding, even when no slur is drawn.—The *Pralltriller* " ought " to be indicated by the sign

(After P. E. Bach.)

The fourth edition of Löhlein's work appeared in 1782; the third of Em. Bach's in 1787. In 1789 Daniel Gottlob Türk, Musical Director at Halle University, published his " Pianoforte-Method " (Clavierschule), an excellent work, containing perhaps the most convenient general view of matters appertaining to piano-playing, in the second half of the eighteenth century, that one can consult. From the Notes one likewise learns Türk's sources, which he critically elucidates. Thus he repudiates, in the very first paragraph on the trill, the term " principal

tone," employed by some ("though not quite correctly") to distinguish
the lower tone; he would prefer the term "written tone." Of course,
the trill does not begin on the "written tone, but on the auxiliary
tone," as the examples show:

In §34 he says, literally: "Every common trill usually begins on the
auxiliary (*a*); hence, the execution at *b* would be incorrect:

He also finds the indication of the auxiliary by a short appoggiatura,
superfluous; "even without it, the trill would begin [in his examples]
on the auxiliary."

Examples:

"In case an appoggiatura is intended to fill half the time-value of the
tone, this must be precisely indicated." Examples:

"These are the . . . tied trills, in which, after an appoggiatura,
or, instead of that, after a slurred note (*c*), the first tone of the trill is
tied."

Can these be the exceptional cases, which Türk had in mind, for
the beginning on the principal tone? We should not designate them
as such; for even though the principal tone is the first trill-tone that
one hears, the trill none the less really begins on the auxiliary, tied
though it be.

Respecting the half-trill (short trill), or *Pralltriller*, Türk follows Em. Bach.

The circumstance that the tied notes *d* and *c* (at *b*) "are not heard,* unquestionably occasioned the adoption of the more convenient, abbreviated notation (*c*). If we consider that this embellishment is at bottom merely an abbreviated trill without after-beat, we shall find the notation at *b* or + correcter than that at *c*, because the common trill begins on the auxiliary."

The "snapping" of the penultimate note in the *Pralltriller*, also recommended by Em. Bach, he indicates by a comma:

Em. Bach's description (X, §34) is similar: "For this reason, when it, the *Pralltriller*, occurs on a note under a *fermata*, the appoggiatura is made very long, and this trill is snapped off at the close, the finger being lifted from the key."

In the employment of the *Pralltriller* he follows Marpurg, and goes still further, saying that "even the best composers sometimes permit themselves one exception or another in this matter":

etc., etc.

From the foregoing the conviction will have been reached, that in the second half of the eighteenth century, and therefore during Beethoven's youth, the beginning of the trill on its auxiliary was the

---

* Here Türk seeks to controvert Agricola.

rule, at least among German musicians,* while the beginning on the principal note was an exception not even recognized by all.

We have to note some further exceptions, though prescribed only for special cases, at the dividing-line between the eighteenth and nineteenth centuries, formulated by the Italian, Muzio Clementi, and his pupil, J. B. Cramer. Clementi's " Introduction to the Art of Playing the Pianoforte" (Einleitung in die Kunst, das Pianoforte zu spielen, " translated from the English"; New, improved edition, Leipzig, au Bureau de Musique. A. Kühnel †), contains examples of trills which are interesting to us.

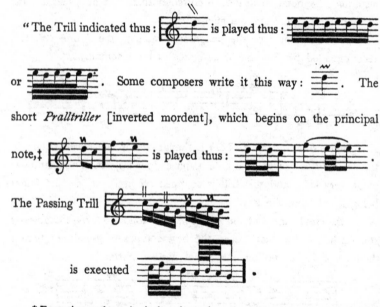

" The Trill indicated thus :   is played thus :

or   . Some composers write it this way :   . The

short *Pralltriller* [inverted mordent], which begins on the principal

note,‡   is played thus :

The Passing Trill

is executed

---

* Excepting perhaps Agricola, whose views do not impress us as quite plain.

† The separate text in notes has the register 104, being the same as that of the old, or earliest, edition published; " Wien, bei Hoffmeister & Comp. Leipzig im Bureau de Musique von Hoffmeister und Kühnel."—According to C. F. Becker, the Clementi Method was published by Pleyel at Paris in 1801; an augmented and improved edition, 1802.—Another edition, in oblong form : "Vollständige Klavierschule," etc., publ. at Vienna by Cappi & Comp., Graben No. 1,112 (register 1,225), probably appeared later.

‡ In the earlier edition mentioned above, only " Der kurze Anschlagstriller, der, etc."

It is sometimes written out in small notes, *e.g.*,  .

This trill may properly be considered as a *Pralltriller*." [This last sentence is omitted in the earlier edition.]

"The trill with turn: 

is played as follows:  or sometimes thus:  .

The long, ordinary trill, 

is executed  .

The prepared trill, 

is executed 

.

The trill with a slur* from the preceding note

is played:

"

* The slur is omitted (probably by mistake) in the earlier edition.—Similar exceptional beginnings of the trill are also found in the "Pianoforte-Method of the Paris Conservatory," edited by L. Adam. (From a German edition by Breitkopf & Härtel. The original was published, according to C. F. Becker, by Sieber at Paris, 1798.)

[The upper example may also be executed thus:]

Down to this last example, and the one which we mark with N.B., there is no material change from the earlier treatment of the beginning of the trill.*

Schindler remarks Beethoven's "appreciation of the short, concise method by the aged Clementi," which he recommended to his friend, Stephen von Breuning, for the latter's son. (It appears that at that time—in or after 1825—it was not procurable in Vienna. [Biography, 3d ed., II, 183].) However, Beethoven seems not to have made the acquaintance of this method until that time †; at all events, it would

---

* Here, too, we should hardly perceive any difference in principle, if the note preceding the trill were written in the form of an appoggiatura. *Cf.* Couperin, Quantz, and J. S. Bach's "Accent und Trillo" (short trill with suspension).

† Beethoven writes to v. Breuning: "Do not take the piano-method by Czerny [N. B.—Joseph Czerny. His method was published, according to Nohl, by Haslinger, in 1825] for the present. I shall get detailed information about another in a few days." And again, "Herewith I send the promised Clementi method." (Nohl: "Beethoven's Letters," 1865, p. 323, *et seq.*) Part I of the sixth revised edition of J. Czerny's "Wiener Clavierlehrer," which is before us, refers but briefly to the trill: "It begins on the higher or lower auxiliary, according as the composer indicates or wishes it to be executed. In the following chain of trills, each begins on the higher auxiliary, and to each the close is added:"

For the rest, according to Schindler [Biogr., 3d ed., II, 182], Joseph Czerny was Carl Czerny's successor as the teacher of Beethoven's nephew. According to Nohl ["Beethoven's Letters," 1865, p. 129], Carl Czerny began teaching the nephew in [about the end of?] 1815.—Later [before 1821?] Friedrich Starke also occupied this position [Nohl: "Beethoven nach den Schilderungen seiner Zeitgenossen," p. 147].

be hasty to conclude that he approved of the above elucidations of the trill without exception.

An English edition of J. B. Cramer's " Anweisung das Pianoforte zu spielen," published by Chappel & Co. (No. 77), probably appeared somewhat later.* For convenience' sake we quote from a German edition (Peters). Cramer's gives his directions for the trill only in the form of Notes appended to short exercises. In his first example of a trill, he plants himself squarely on Em. Bach's standpoint:

To this he adds the Note: " . . . The trill begins on the higher tone, and finishes on the principal tone, because it is usually followed by an after-beat. . . . ." The "transient or short shake" in the annexed "Hungarian air,"

is to be executed thus:

[That is, half Clementi, half L. Mozart.]

* "J. B. Cramer's Instructions for the Pianoforte, etc., etc."—In it the compass of the keyboard is given as from contra-*F* to *c*⁴, with the remark that pianos had recently (then) been constructed with a range of 6 octaves (contra-*F* to *f*⁴); but these latter were not in general use.—On the other hand, a reporter for the Leipzig "Musikalische Zeitung" of 1816 says, in discussing a new (German) edition of the Piano-Method, published by Breitkopf & Härtel, that this method for beginners "has been known longer than, and almost as well as, his grand exercises for advanced players." Book I of Cramer's Études may be referred, with considerable confidence, to the end of the eighteenth century.

However, with the trill which "stands on the higher note of a chord," Cramer invades modern territory. For example, the trill in Haydn's "Kaiser Hymn," *

etc.

should be executed thus:

[!]

On the other hand, J. L. Dussek's "Clavierschule" (translated from the English edition, and published in a revised and augmented edition by the author—Leipzig: Breitkopf & Härtel [1st ed., 1803, acc. to C. F. Becker †])—teaches the beginning of the trill only in the old fashion:

"The trill without after-beat [notation] is played [notation];

Trill with after-beats [notation] thus: [notation];

[notation] thus:

[notation] [!]; and [notation]

* But this trill occurs neither in the hymn proper ("sung for the first time February 12, 1797"), nor in the so-called "Kaiserquartette." The passage reads, both times, in notes: [notation] (In the Quartette finally in the higher octave.)

† The English original appeared, according to Becker, under the title "Instructions on the Art of Playing the Piano Forte," in London, 1796.

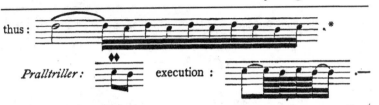

thus :

Pralltriller : execution :

In general, however, the old views retained full validity among German theorists everywhere during the first decades of the nineteenth century; *e.g.,* in the "Klavier- und Fortepianoschule," by A. E. Müller (Jena, 1804), the sixth thoroughly revised (or, rather, recast †) edition of Löhlein's. He gives the trill :

to be executed

;

without after-beat , execution as before. "Many composers also employ in this case the sign *tr*, then writing out" the after-beat. —Further, the trill with appoggiatura, which latter may be " short without change," or "long without change"—("in the latter case it takes its entire time-value ") :

* His Study on Trills in Thirds

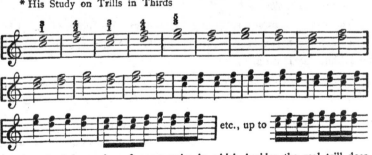

etc., up to

may be regarded as only a finger-exercise, in which, besides, the real trill does not occur.

† According to the editor's Preface, only Part II of Löhlein's work, treating on Thoroughbass, remained.

Trill with double appoggiatura; sign "or, more frequently":

and sometimes  "The double

appoggiatura is always to be played as rapidly as the trill itself; *e.g.:*

Written :   Executed :

He gives the *Pralltriller* ("short, or half-, trill") thus: *

executed : †

For the interpretation of the sign "*tr*" in printed music of that time, the following remark is important: "Now-a-days, particularly in engraved music, the sign *tr* is also employed to indicate the *Pralltriller*,

as  where it is impossible to play any

trill but the *Pralltriller*.

The same examples, excepting the last, are also given in the little "Elementarbuch für Klavierspieler" by A. E. Müller, published later by Kühnel at Leipzig.

The "Méthode pour le Piano-Forté" by D. Steibelt (b. Berlin, 1765), "Français avec la traduction allemande" (Offenbach chez J. André,

---

* Here a slight misprint in the original is corrected in the Errata.

† Here we correct a slight misprint not noticed among the Errata :

 This same mistake also appears in Müller's little elementary

treatise.

No. 2,770), likewise remains faithful to German principles regarding the beginning of the trill:

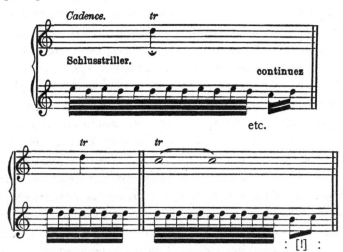

"Études pour la double trille avec la main droite:

" etc.

Finally we notice the "Wiener Pianoforte-Schule" by Friedrich Starke, 1819, for Part II of which (1820) Beethoven provided with fingering his Andante and Rondo from the Sonata op. 28.

"The ordinary Trill:

Evidently Ph. E. Bach's principles.

The first who, as he himself asserts, intentionally reversed this old rule for beginning the trill, and established the beginning of the ordinary trill on the principal note, was J. N. Hummel, in his "Ausführliche theoretisch-practische Anweisung zum Pianoforte-Spiel," published in 1828, a year after Beethoven's death. (Vienna, 1828: Tobias Haslinger. The Preface was dated "Weimar, December, 1827.")

Let us hear the leader of fashion in *our* century.—"With respect to the trill the old practice has hitherto obtained, of always beginning it with the higher auxiliary; this was probably founded on the first elementary rules for singing. . . ."—If these words were literally true, there could be no more doubt concerning Beethoven's practice! Or does not Hummel intend to claim "priority of invention," but merely consider himself the first publicly to announce this principle? *—To proceed: "Two principal reasons decide me to lay down the rule, that, in general, every trill ought to begin on that note over which it stands, and not (unless specially indicated) on the higher auxiliary:

"(*a*) Because the principal tone, which is usually followed by a sort of closing tone, should strike the ear more sharply than the auxiliary, and the tone-accent should fall on the accented beat, *i.e.*, on the trill-tone (+):

Execution:

"(*b*) Because the successions of tones are different, on the piano, from those on other instruments; and the order of our fingers, dependent on the position of the hands, usually renders it more convenient to commence the trill (1) on the principal tone rather than (2) on the

* He recommends the following "trill-exercise with all five fingers alternately, which Mozart showed [me] how to play":

According to this, even W. A. Mozart had already begun the trill on the principal note.

auxiliary; for in the latter case, executing the trill from above downward, the player is often obliged to raise the hand, or to substitute
another finger on the same key, *e.g.,*

to be executed:

rather than

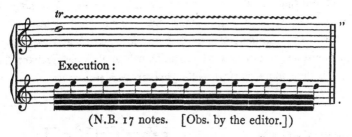

At * the finger passing over falls naturally into place on the trill-note;
at ** one has first to raise the finger, and then substitute the third
finger."—"The trill, therefore, generally begins on the principal note,
and always ends on it:

(N.B. 17 notes.   [Obs. by the editor.])

" Where the trill is to begin on the higher or lower auxiliary, this
must be indicated by a corresponding grace-note:

[N.B. 16 Notes.]

[16 Notes here also.]

(* On the next page this grace-note is crossed :

etc.)

A third reason for beginning the trill on the principal note was discovered by Fr. Kalkbrenner. His "Anweisung das Pianoforte mit
Hülfe des Handleiters spielen zu lernen" (op. 108) was published in
German and French at Leipzig by Kistner in 1832. [?] ("A Paris
chez l'Auteur.")

As trill-sign, Kalkbrenner is familiar with *tr* or ⌒ . Touching the
execution he says (p. 38) : "Trills must be practised slowly at first,
then with gradually increasing rapidity, and in *crescendo* and *decrescendo*.
They must begin and end on the principal note, as the resultant harmony is then more satisfactory; composers sometimes desire, for special reasons [!], to have them begin on the higher or lower auxiliary,

indicating either by a small note : 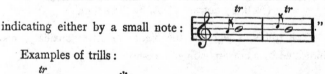 "

Examples of trills :

* *F* and *f²*, supporting-fingers.

68

Further:

"Trill by John Field."

Here we see that "more satisfactory harmony" is the reason for forsaking the earlier system.

On testing these reasons according to their intrinsic value, that advanced by Kalkbrenner, "satisfactory harmony," appears null and void.

"However, one can observe that Dissonances are generally played stronger, and Consonances weaker," said Ph. E. Bach [see Part II of our Preface].

The same assertion is made by Türk (Chap. VI, §32). Consequently, this accentuation, this emphasizing of dissonances is, according to the testimony of such acute and scientifically trained theorists as Ph. E. Bach and Türk, a beauty.—In point of fact, such a trill as

sounds empty and weak in contrast with the following "snappy" one:

and this difference is caused precisely by the predominance of consonance or dissonance on the accented beats. (*Cf.* Marpurg's explanation of the trill, page 43.)

But how is it when a chord takes, for example, this form:

Here, although the highest tone, to be sure, is consonant with both the inner part and the fundamental, it is an element foreign to the chord as a whole, and thus, in the wider sense of the term, a dissonance. (We will admit, on the other hand, that the leading-tone as such has a certain priority.)

From the close of Beethoven's Variations in E♭ major, op. 35, we can perceive how little he tried to avoid a dissonance in a trill—that he, in fact, rather sought for dissonant effects:

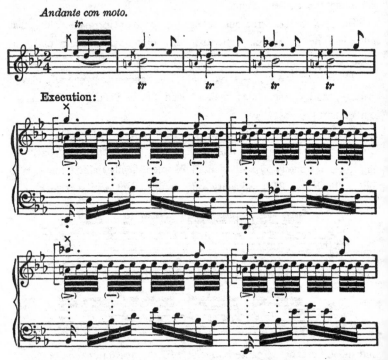

Now, as to Hummel's reasons, the second ("ease of execution") is too purely external to affect the nature of the trill. The lifting of the hand might have an unpleasing effect in the given passage:

which could, however, be readily obviated by tying the two tones at the point of meeting:

But, with reference to Hummel's other reason, "special prominence of the principal note,* more particularly in consideration of the following closing note," we will concede that for this some justification might be found.   But let us first hear Carl Czerny.

It would argue strong prepossession to absolutely identify with Hummel's theory of the trill that set forth by Czerny in his " Complete Theoretico-practical Pianoforte-Method " (in 3 parts; op. 500; Vienna : Ant. Diabelli & Co., *circa* 1810), Part I.   Czerny was, perhaps, influenced by Hummel, and, like him, commences by letting the trill begin on the principal note; but he cites so many exceptions that we can hardly consider his rules as still maintaining a settled principle. Moreover, in practice he differs further from Hummel in his division of the measure, as we shall prove by an example further on.

True, his first example of the trill coincides at all points with Hummel :

also his chain of trills :

* According to Marpurg, the principal tone was specially accented at the end of the trill.

Execution :

But the commencement of the trill on the principal note occurs (for the present, only) "when the trill was preceded either by nothing at all, or by some note which is different from its principal note, and is, therefore, played on another key."

On the other hand, the trill always begins on the auxiliary "when the trill is immediately preceded by the same tone as its principal note." *E.g.,*

Such cases, however, are by no means rare.—Another exception, given only in the example (on chromatic signs in the trill), is found in the following chain of trills:

The first trill (7 notes) begins on the principal note; the second (for it is, in fact, a new trill [*cf.* explanations by Walther *et al.*]), on the auxiliary (8 notes); the third again on the principal note; and the fourth, in turn, on the auxiliary. Apart from the resulting difficulty of evenness in execution, what inconsistency! We find the latter again in another example, which is intended to demonstrate the decreasing rapidity of a *morendo* trill:

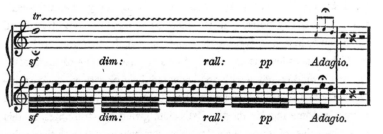

Here, to be sure, we have "strong emphasis" of the fundamental, making the latter "strike the ear more sharply" than all the following tones; and herewith Hummel's requirement would seem to be fulfilled; but, commencing with the very next beat, our trill (barring the ugly *fermata*) looks as decorous as any early classic trill.

In like manner Czerny, in his "160 Eight-measure Exercises," op. 821, No. 5, arranged a trill for beginners:

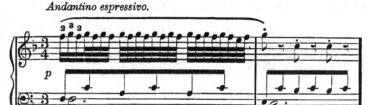

Was it a reminiscence of his youth that guided him?—This question we shall answer further on.

Now let us examine a modern trill more closely. It begins and ends on the principal note. In every case it consists of an odd number of notes, and in this respect is not altered in the least by the addition of the usual after-beat; *e.g.,*

equal to $8 \times 2 + 1$, or 17 notes; or, taking away the after-beat, $7 \times 2 + 1$, or 15 notes. As it would be difficult to apportion these seventeen or fifteen to two quarter-notes so evenly, that each trill-note would be just as long as any other (in which case not one of them, after the first, would coincide with any accented beat or with an accompaniment divided in accordance with such beats), we are obliged to take refuge in some regular mode of division, giving the trill-notes, in this case, the value of thirty-seconds. But somewhere, either at the beginning or the end, (for no other place would appear rational,) there will now be formed a group of three notes.*

Here the modern theory of the trill splits into two systems; the one, Kalkbrenner-Hummel's, locates the triplet at the end of the trill; while the other, which Czerny only partially, and perhaps only instinctively, upholds, sets the triplet at the beginning of the trill.†

* The other possible method of division, namely into triplets, would also fail, in the case of seventeen notes, to bring about full uniformity of the groups :

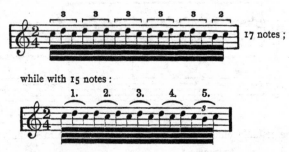

we should have to count five eighth-notes against four; which again renders a rational division practically impossible.

† E. D. Wagner, in his " Musical Ornamentation " (Musikalische Ornamen

The latter procedure, however, is almost identical with the earlier system, from which it differs only in the first three notes :

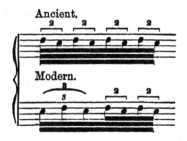

whereas the former is diametrically opposed to it up to the very last moment.   Now, we have already observed that we consider the peculiarity, the " beauty " of the earlier trill to reside precisely in the predominance of the dissonance—in the coincidence of the auxiliary with the strong beats.   Consequently, when a trill begins, for any reason, on the principal tone—and such cases also occurred in the works of the earlier composers !—we should prefer to start with a triplet, then carrying out the rest of the trill in groups of two notes ; thus, for the remainder of the trill, not departing in the least from the fundamental idea of the earlier theory.   This method might, perhaps, be recommended for such trills as seem to necessitate a deviation from the old fundamental rule.   In many cases, however, especially in rather short trills, this procedure will be found inconvenient on account of the change in rhythm, and we shall then prefer the trill according to Ph. E. Bach.

How strongly Czerny himself was still influenced by the earlier

tik ; Berlin : Schlesinger), proceeds somewhat differently in forming the beginning of his " Trill *ex abrupto*," not with a triplet, but with a *Pralltriller :*

(page 197)  etc.

This excellent work contains a clear view of the science of embellishment according to Ph. E. Bach, Türk, Marpurg, etc., with practical examples, and arrives at original conclusions.

method, is seen in his accompanied trills. We cite, to begin with, the
following trill with single sustained notes :

and then, with a melody, quite in accord with the old school :

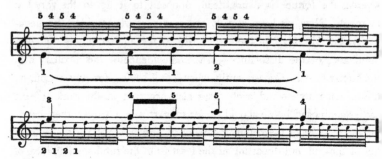

" But when these melody-notes are difficult to stretch, they are to be
struck alone, omitting the principal note [of the trill].   But each melody-
note must then be followed by the principal note ; *e.g.:*

That is, the auxiliary notes in this case (excepting the not quite intelligible beginning) coincide with the strong beats.

We skip the various further modifications. But, before closing this chapter, we must notice Czerny's *Pralltriller*, or "*Schneller*,"

 Execution:

with the appended Note: "The two small notes are played with extreme rapidity, the accent falling on the third note, which has a large note-head." And he illustrates this direction, in the Supplement to his Method, by the following passage from Beethoven's D-minor Sonata: "The *Pralltriller* are to be executed thus:

(etc.)

the principal note being sharply emphasized after the two small notes." Now, as the *Pralltriller* (as in the earlier method) must be proportionately distributed in the measure and "among the accompaniment-notes of the bass," *e.g.*:

etc.; (example from Czerny)

this passage, according to Czerny, could hardly be otherwise performed than

Such an accentuation, totally disregarding all rhythmic feeling, can surely not be ascribed to Beethoven. Either Czerny heard the accent correctly, in which case Beethoven played thus:

or Beethoven divided the notes as Czerny requires, but accented thus:

Now, in what manner did Beethoven begin his ordinary trill?—We have seen, that during his childhood and youth the theory of beginning on the auxiliary was, at least in Germany, predominant or most prominent, although certain theorists admitted some modifications or deviations (probably only apparent ones, in part). We have also learned, that this earlier theory, apart from Cramer-Clementi's exceptional cases, was still in vogue early in the nineteenth century (Müller, Dussek, Starke [1819]). Finally, we heard from Hummel, in words which he probably wrote down in the very year of Beethoven's death, that in this point the old method still held its own. But, from all this evidence, we cannot conclude apodictically that this last point holds good in Beethoven's case.

If we inquire concerning his teachers, it may be assumed that his father already taught him to trill; as to the latter's course of study and artistic usages, the editor has no information. Should we venture a conjecture, we might possibly assume that Beethoven's father, a singer by profession, was likely to have been taught after Tosi's method. But just Tosi's views on the trill [see page 41]—not to mention Agricola's (whose translation appeared when B.'s father was 17)—strike

the editor, at least, as far less explicit than the plain directions of
Walther or Ph. E. Bach. On the other hand, to be sure, the youthful
Ludwig might have learned more exact rules for the trill from L.
Mozart's Violin-method—supposing his instruction to have been based
upon it. As to all this, we know nothing. Touching his later teachers,
van den Eeden and Pfeiffer, there is greater probability that they were
adherents of Ph. E. Bach's principles; and, finally, we know of Neefe
that he himself was "educated in the strict Leipzig school," and likewise that he taught his pupil, Beethoven, according to Ph. E. Bach's
school. But, even admitting that Neefe himself was thoroughly at
home in Ph. E. Bach's "Manieren," would he, with such an advanced
pupil, have troubled himself about details like the execution of a trill ?
Besides, we must take note of the fact that in 1762 a Second Part had
been added to Bach's "Versuch über die wahre Art, das Clavier zu
spielen," containing, under the above collective title, a "Lehre von
dem Accompagnement und der freyen Fantasie" [Method for Accompaniment and the Free Fantasia], *i.e.*, the art of playing figured basses,
of "elegant" accompaniment, and other matters relating to style* and
extempore playing. Would not these have been of greater interest to
the youthful Beethoven than the instructions in Part I for fingering and
for playing the embellishments ? And was it, perhaps, only the Second
Part from which the teacher instructed his pupil ?—According to
Cramer's Magazin [Thayer, I, 120], "Herr Neefe also gave him some
instruction in thoroughbass."

That Beethoven was, however, also acquainted with Part I of Bach's
"Versuch," may be quite confidently inferred from the circumstance
that later, with his pupil Czerny, he began after the very first lessons
with the study of the exercises belonging to this part.† Although

*We add, to prevent misunderstanding, that the instructions on style refer
especially to the accompaniment, and are, in a degree, merely supplementary to
those which the author had already given (in Part I, to which he refers) concerning "Handsachen."

†Nohl, according to Czerny's report. ["Beethoven nach den Schilderungen
seiner Zeitgenossen," by Ludwig Nohl, p. 32.] There are eighteen "trial pieces"
(*Probestücke*) in six sonatas; augmented by eight further piano-pieces in the third
edition.

these "trial pieces" are printed (with the other examples in notes for Part I) on special plates in folio, it would appear necessary to refer to the letterpress explanations of the numerous "Manieren" (embellishments).

True, one might be perfectly familiar with Bach's "Manieren," without subscribing to them in every point; and with regard to the trill, in particular, there is hardly any circumstance which could so shake belief in the identity of Beethoven's trill with that of Bach, as the following:

Any one who has attentively read Ph. E. Bach's directions for the trill can hardly have failed to notice the sentence: ". . . consequently,

the practice of indicating it [the trill] by a grace-note

[Plate IV, Fig. XXIII, *d.*] is superfluous, unless this grace-note is to be treated like an appoggiatura." Now, it is likely that various grace-notes, representing the higher auxiliary to the trill, have been smuggled later into the editions of Beethoven's piano-works, *e. g.*, the single appoggiatura in the last movement of op. 7 in the Czerny-Simrock edition:

 In other piano-works, however, they were

doubtless written by the composer himself, though they appear seldom and (*nota bene*) always in the shape of short appoggiaturas. Such are, as we may assume with considerable or entire confidence, those in the original editions of op. 2, No. 3 [Artaria, 614]

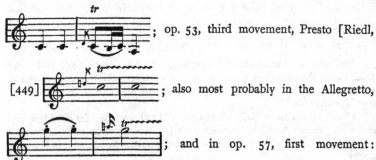

; op. 53, third movement, Presto [Riedl,

[449] ; also most probably in the Allegretto,

; and in op. 57, first movement:

. Further, in the pianoforte-con-

certo arranged from the violin-concerto, op. 61 [Bureau des Arts,

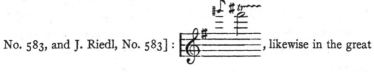

No. 583, and J. Riedl, No. 583] : , likewise in the great

B♭-major Trio, op. 97, first movement (once) :

[Steiner & Comp., 2582.]

(None of the shorter trills immediately preceding have the appoggiatura.)

Now, these examples of Beethoven's trill-notation exhibit, apart from their rarity, the peculiarity that they are usually employed in cases where the auxiliary is provided with a chromatic sign; and in the first example the appoggiatura may possibly be intended to prevent the substitution of a *Pralltriller* for the trill [*cf.* p. 54]; but the composer had other means of indicating the chromatic sign for the auxiliary (♭*tr*).

To explain this (in any event) rare phenomenon, either of two hypotheses might be chosen: (1) It may have been a transient style of notation (and Ph. E. Bach's warning seems to prove that the notation of the auxiliary trill-note by means of a grace-note had been no infrequent occurrence); or (2) it may have been a precautionary measure to prevent the beginning of the trill on the principal note. But why take such measures at a time when a composer might well take it for granted that the old-fashioned way of beginning the trill was the regular and popular one? Did not Hummel say, in 1828, that in this point the old method still held its own? Hummel could certainly not have adopted his ideas concerning the trill at the moment of writing them

down, but after trying them for a considerable time or after comparing them with the opinions or practice of other musicians. In fact, we
are in a position, through the foresight of our publisher, to show that
Hummel's theory in all probability matured very early, and that his
dictum would, therefore, have reference only to instruction-books with
which he was acquainted. We have received an oblong edition of
Hummel's op. 8, "*XIII Variazioni . . . sopra una Canzonetta
nazionale austriaca. . . . In Vienna presso Artaria* * (No. 879),"
probably published at the beginning of the nineteenth century, whose
dainty theme runs thus:

has the following fingering for the trill in the fifth variation:

It appears, therefore, that Hummel established his principles for the
trill at the outset, and consistently maintained them; and his example
was very likely to have found speedy imitation, while his practice can
scarcely have remained unnoticed by Beethoven.

Should any one care to set up a third hypothesis (which is not incon-
ceivable in the light of the foregoing remarks), that Beethoven began
with the higher auxiliary only such trills as are preceded by the said
auxiliary in the form of a short appoggiatura, and consequently usually

---

* Strangely enough, "et Comp." is omitted; but the register, 879, agrees exactly with that of a recent catalogue of the firm of "Artaria et Comp." The entire title follows: "*XIII Variazioni / con aggiunta di Coda in fine / Composte sopra
una Canzonetta nazionale austriaca / per il / Clavicembalo o Forte-Piano / e dedicate
al Illustrissimo / Sig. Barone Carlo Augusto di Lichstenstein / da / Giov: Nep: Hummel di Vienna* [!] *Op. 8. / In Vienna presso Artaria.* / [To the left] *879* [rather in-
distinct]. [To the right] *f. 1.* [Inside] *879* [even once upside down at the upper
edge of the plate!]. The very thick paper, yellow from age, and the "Hummel
di Vienna," show that the copy must be very old—printed (judging by the register-number) about 1801.

trilled *à la* Hummel, we shall now confront him with a number of passages which prove, apparently, that such an assumption is void. We have already drawn attention to the difference between the trill-theories of Hummel and Czerny; we have frequently cited the latter as an important witness in matters pertaining to Beethoven's art; and Czerny's testimony shall again be quoted (with reserve) to show Beethoven's way of beginning the trill—but this time not in his character as author of the great Pianoforte-Method, op. 500! To be sure, the editor at one time considered the trill-theories therein contained to have a certain validity for Beethoven's works, as well; this was during his editorial work on the Eb–Major Concerto, the first of the five to be finished. But various indications and observations soon filled him more and more with a legitimate distrust. Thus (to notice only one instance) Czerny gives, in the Supplement to his Pianoforte-Method, the oft-cited " Kunst des Vortrags," the following directions for Beethoven's G-major Concerto :

" The closing trill with the following fingering : "

Now, these trill-appoggiaturas were added by Czerny; they are found neither in the original edition [Kunst- und Industriecomptoir No. 592] nor in the edition published by T. Haslinger after Beethoven's death [No. 8547]. And when the left hand, in the next measure, also passes

into the trill :  it will not take up the

trill in the contrary way from the right hand, but in the same way :

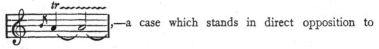 ,—a case which stands in direct opposition to

Czerny's teachings.

How great was our astonishment, however, when we finally found an arrangement by Czerny of the Variations from Beethoven's " Kreutzer

Sonata" (op. 47) for pianoforte solo, and in an edition by Diabelli et Comp. (No. 1168 *), which, although not itself the first edition, must have appeared, judging by the inside register-number (C. et D. No. 1168), during Beethoven's lifetime (perhaps about 1821), in which Czerny's later trill-theory is transformed into its opposite! Many of the trills in this edition are provided with double fingering, the first appearing in measure 24 *et seq.*,

There are, beside, many other passages in which the execution of the trills is indicated, either by the fingering or by added grace-notes; for example, in the theme:

* Variations brillantes/tirées de l'Oeuvre 47/de/Louis van Beethoven,/ arrangées pour le Piano-Forte/seul/par/Charles Czerny./Vienne/chez A. Diabelli* et Comp./Graben No. 1133./[To the left] No. 1168.   [To the right] Pr. 1 f. 15 x.C.M.   [Inside] C. et D. No. 1168.—The publishing-house of "Cappi et Diabelli" (Diabelli became Peter Cappi's partner in 1818) changed the firm-name [Notte-bohm: "Beethoveniana," p. 47] in 1824 to "A. Diabelli u. Comp."   Beethoven's op. 120 was published by Cappi u. Diabelli in June, 1823, with the register-number 1380.

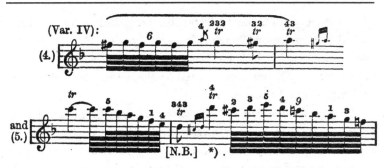

furthermore :

(At × × the figures stand beside the notes, not over the *tr*.)

and finally, in the Coda :

and, 12 measures before the close :

(Other trills, *e.g.*, in Var. I, have neither fingering nor grace-notes.)

From analysis of these styles of trill-notation we obtain the following

---

*4 3 ?—The 3 was probably merely forgotten after the 4 ; this may be assumed from the position of the 4, and also from the following fingering, which precludes the idea of " 4 5."

rule: They begin on the auxiliary; the exceptions, which we have marked N. B., are generally referable to the case (which must be the most natural one) in which the higher auxiliary itself immediately precedes the *tr*. (*Cf.* examples 1, 5, and 6; the last one, to be sure, may be interpreted in the contrary mode.)

These variations were later incorporated into Czerny's "Art of Fingering," in which they represent the 11th Book. [Vienna: A. Diabelli & Comp.; register-number D. et C. No. 1168.*] The fingering, in so far as it concerns our present examples, remained unchanged.

The matter assumes a totally different aspect, however, when we examine the score-edition of the Kreutzer Sonata, by Czerny-Simrock.† Here, as in the Czerny-Simrock edition of the pianoforte-sonatas, the trill-fingering is indicated by only one figure, and all additional notes, like those in examples 1, 4, 7, and 8, are omitted. In one place, however, the editor was obliged to employ a double fingering (Var. 4, p. 26, meas. 12–14); this passage is fingered thus:

From the double fingerings marked ×, which owe their origin simply to the circumstance that two neighboring fingers are not employed in these places, we clearly see that the editor requires that all should begin on the principal note. But if we compare with these trills the last trill in our preceding example No. 6, something else becomes evident: *Czerny had changed his opinion!* It may not be without interest to trace the history of this change.

---

* Therefore, only a reprint from the old plates.

† *Edition revue, corrigée metronomisée et doigtee par Ch. Czerny. Bonn chez N. Simrock.* (Complete Edition of the violin-sonatas.) We can supply no information on the age of this still current edition. The register-number, 422, is the same as in the original edition. It was N. Simrock's custom to retain the same number for later, newly engraved editions.

Beethoven's Piano Playing

Czerny's instruction under Beethoven, which began toward the end of 1800, appears not to have been very regular, and to have been interrupted "after a time." * Czerny had, therefore, to depend in part on self-instruction. On the other hand, "he profited much by his acquaintance with . . . Hummel, whose playing opened a new world to him, and with Clementi, whose method of teaching he studied." [Grove: "Dictionary."] From the latter's piano-method Czerny might readily have learned the earlier modes of playing the trill, with but few modifications, in case Beethoven had given him no direct instructions. †
Moreover, in 1825, ‡ he figures as the editor of the eighth edition of A. E. Müller's "Grosse Pianoforteschule," already mentioned above. We do not know how he treated the trill in this work; but it will suffice to examine his work as editor of the small "Elementarbuch" by A. E. Müller. § Here we read, on the trill:

"Its sign is this, *tr*, and as a rule it begins on the higher auxiliary. But it may also begin on the lower tone [principal note], and sometimes the lower auxiliary may begin; *e.g.*,

* "And I was therefore again left to depend on my own industry." (Communicated by Czerny to Nohl.) When he played to Nohl Beethoven's sonatas op. 53 (publ. in May, 1805), *a vista* from the manuscript, he had not seen Beethoven, as he himself relates, for two years. [Nohl: "Beethoven nach den Schilderungen seiner Zeitgenossen," p. 33.]

† In 1805 was publ. (acc. to Grove) his op. 1 : Variations for Pianoforte and Violin on a theme by Krumbholz. (We have only a second edition of this.) In 1818 Cappi & Diabelli publ. his op. 2, Rondo *à 4 mains*.

‡ Acc. to C. F. Becker's "Systematisch-chronologisches Darstellung der musikalischen Litteratur," 1836.

§ "Kleines Elementarbuch für Klavierspieler," by August Eberhard Müller. New edition, with additions by Carl Czerny. Leipzig, au Bureau de Musique von C. F. Peters. Price, 1 Thlr. 20 Ngr. Oblong, without register. [After 1828?] Müller died in 1817 as Hofkapellmeister at Weimar.

Second Example:
Written:

Played:

(and):

It is evident that here, as well as with the turn, the preceding tone may determine the tone on which the trill begins."

It is hard to say what influence caused Czerny to formulate the theory of the trill as found in his great Pianoforte-Method, op. 500; presumably, however, it was the great authority of Hummel which finally moved him, directly or indirectly, to support this theory. Only a short time before the publication of Hummel's "Clavierschule" (1828) we find him laboring, by means of a lengthy exercise, to promote the development of dexterity in trilling *according to the earlier method!* Czerny's op. 146 is a Funeral March on the death of Beethoven—hence it belongs to 1827. Probably in the same year appeared his "Great Trill-exercise in the form of a brilliant Rondo for the Pianoforte, op. 151." "Wien bey Anton Diabelli u. Comp." Register 2793.* This piece forms the 21st Book of his "Art of Fingering," from which edition we quote (it is possibly only a reprint; the register reads "D. et C. No. 2792). On p. 4 we find, preceding the musical text, some

Observations.

"No. 1. As a trill may begin in three ways, namely, on the higher, on the middle, and on the lower tone:

---

* Beethoven's op. 129 (œuvre posthume) was publ. by A. Diabelli & Comp. in Jan., 1828, with the register-number 2819. [Nottebohm.]

the rule holds good, that in this exercise it shall always begin in the first mode (on the higher key). No. 2. But where several trills occur in succession, descending, each must begin in the second mode (on the middle key, or principal note) ; *e.g.,*

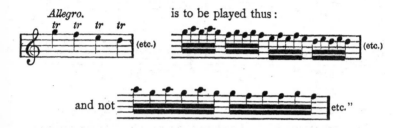

is to be played thus :

and not

As we see, the familiar exception for the familiar reasons.*

Returning after this digression to Czerny's contributions to Beethoven literature, we shall bring forward some further items calculated to throw an important light on the master's practice—only, to be sure, in case we are able to regard them as resulting from careful observation or precise knowledge of the master's usages : a point on which we offer no opinion. Thus, Czerny's op. 61, " Preludes, Cadences and Little Fantasias in the brilliant style " [" Präludien, Cadenzen und kleine Fantasien im brillanten Style . . ." (A. Diabelli & Comp., No. 1424)], contains a " Cadence to the First Movement of Beethoven's Concerto

---

* Besides, despite the observations, numerous trills are provided with appog-

giaturas, *e.g.*: (etc.) Ditto in the

bass. In the course of the piece, other exceptions likewise occur. Those on p. 10 are clearly engraver's mistakes ; but on p. 12 we find

etc.

in C minor." Besides various trills without grace-notes or fingering, we find at the close:

a case in direct contradiction of the Pianoforte-Method, op. 500.

Yet more interesting are Czerny's arrangements (à 2† and à 4 mains) of Beethoven's C-major Overture, op. 124 ("zur Weihe des Hauses"). In the one-measure Adagio, after the two *fermate* (p. 11 of the 2-hand arr.), Czerny writes:

* According to the Pianoforte-Method, "double trills for one hand . . . are subject to the same rules as simple ones." *E.g.*,

† Ouverture / Oeuvre 124, / de / Louis van Beethoven. / arrangée pour / Piano-Forte / par / Charles Czerny. / No. 2270.—Propriete des Editeurs.—Pr. 1 f 12 xr / Mayence, / chez B. Schott Fils / Editeurs de Musique de S. A. R. le grand Duc de Hesse. The overture was composed, according to Nottebohm, " for the opening of the Josephstädter Theater at the end of September, 1822." Performed October 3, 1822 (according to the Autograph). Published in 1825.

The grace-note, which we mark with an ×, is wanting in the original score.* But this added note does not only conflict with Czerny's later trill-theory, but also with the exception recommended in the earlier instruction-books; though we should state, that the real reason for this exception (maintenance of the legato in a case where the trill is immediately preceded by its higher auxiliary) is disposed of by making the preceding chord staccato. In any event, however, the arranger must have thought that he was acting in accord with the composer's intentions; or he did not fear discovery; or—Beethoven himself added the note as a correction.†(?)

For completeness' sake we shall finally examine the posthumous Rondo in B♭ for pianoforte with orchestral accompaniment, by Beethoven; to which (according to a memorandum by Dr. Sonnleithner

---

* Mayence, chez B. Schott Fils. No. 2262. Title agrees word for word with that given by Nottebohm, excepting the "(3 Trompes)" which he gives in parenthesis, which are wanting in the copy in the Royal Library, and also in Thayer's Chronological Catalogue under the title of the original edition; they were probably merely forgotten by the composer. Thayer adds a declaration by Beethoven, that the piano-arrangements for two and four hands, by Czerny, "in exact agreement with the score," were about to appear. In the copy of the Czerny arrangement in the Royal Library this little appoggiatura, besides, is crossed out with a red pencil (?). In Czerny's four-hand arrangement (Schott, No. 2314) the trill is even provided with appoggiaturas for all three parts (Vl. I, Vl. II, and Viola):

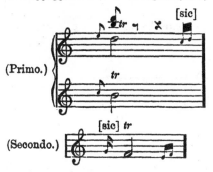

† But see Thayer's Chron. Cat., p. 146 (*ad* op. 124), according to which Beethoven stated that "the piano-arrangements for two and four hands, by Herr Carl Czerny," were "in exact agreement with the score." *Cf.* Beethoven's letter to Czerny of October 8, 1824, in Nohl's "Neue Briefe Beethoven's," p. 274, which letter we believe to refer to this overture only.

based on a statement by Diabelli) Carl Czerny added the close and the accompaniment. [Nottebohm, "Them. Verzeichniss," 2nd ed., p. 142.] This piece, doubtless composed before 1800, perhaps as early as 1795 [*cf.* our Preface to the C-major Concerto; also Nottebohm's Them. Verz., pp. 22 and 142], was published in June, 1829, by A. Diabelli & Comp. Judging by the oblong edition in our possession (probably an original edition),* Czerny did not simply add the close, but likewise editorially revised the entire piano-part. On p. 3 we already find a d^4, on p. 4 an f^4, which Beethoven could not write before 1808-9.—This edition has no fingering, but does contain trills with

appoggiaturas: such as , and also

(N.B. Compare herewith the last example in notes to the G-major

Concerto; and  also without the appog-

---

* Rondeau/en Si♭/pour le/Piano-Forte[1]/composé/par/L. van Beethoven./ Oeuvre posthume./ No. 3251.[2] Propriété des Editeurs. Pr f 1.— C. M./ Vienne, chez Ant. Diabelli et Comp./ Graben No. 1133./ Paris, chez M. Schlesinger.—London, chez Wessel et Stodart.

[1] After "Piano-Forte" Nottebohm interpolates the words "avec accompagnement d'Orchestre"; do they not refer to No. 3252 of this edition?

[2] Our edition has inside the publishers' mark "D. et C. No. 3251. 52." Nottebohm omits the rest of the title, giving "etc." instead.

giatura :

Besides this indirect testimony concerning the execution of Beethoven's trills, for the validity of which we cannot answer, however, we can now mention three cases in his pianoforte-works, in which the author himself clearly expresses his intention, or at least appears to do so. The first, and most unimpeachable, case is connected with the great C-major Sonata, op. 53. We owe our information to the indefatigable searcher after Beethoveniana, the American A. W. Thayer. His " Chronological Catalogue of the Works of Ludwig van Beethoven " (Schneider : Berlin, 1865) contains, among other things relative to op. 53, the following note :

" The MS.* contains the following observations, written by Beethoven's own hand : . . . ' For those who find the trill too difficult where it appears in conjunction with the theme, it may be facilitated as follows :

or taken twice as fast, if ability permits :

Two of these sextuplets are played to every quarter-note in the bass. For the rest, it makes no difference if this trill loses something of its rapidity.' '' [Last page of the manuscript.]

* The manuscript (acc. to Thayer still in the possession of Herr Johann Kaffka of Vienna) is the property of the Imp. R. Councillor Dr. Schebek, of Prague.

This example is indeed instructive. It shows us:

(1) That Beethoven played the auxiliary note of his trill (here, to be sure, only an accompanied trill) on the most strongly accented beat;

(2) That the method of facilitation proposed by Czerny:

did not enter into his mind; and

(3) That it is not likely that he could only "hardly" stretch a tenth; for here he had to strike almost simultaneously

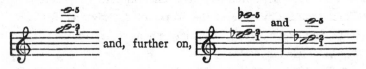

and, further on,

Moreover, in the original manuscript, the trill-passage stands, as written [essentially] by Beethoven, thus:

At × the upper trill-sign is omitted; it is also wanting in the original edition [à Vienne au Bureau des arts et d'industrie, No. 449. Preis 2 fl. 15 x.], of which the library of the "Gesellschaft der Musikfreunde" has but one copy; likewise in later editions, probably from the author's forgetfulness, as will be gathered from the following:

[The slurs indicated by dots were probably also left out by mistake.]

The second case concerns the double trill in the second movement of the Sonata op. 111, published, according to Nottebohm, "by Schlesinger in Berlin (and Paris) in April, 1823.*" We shall first examine the Paris (original) edition of Maurice Schlesinger,† without register-number.

Touching this sonata, Schindler [Biography, 3rd ed., II, p. 3] narrates: "On account of the extraordinary number of errors, even in the second proof, the author requested that op. 111 should be returned to him again, to which the publishers could not consent" [probably on account of the long transit].—This edition is not yet provided with a trill-fingering, which is, however, found in an oblong edition (No. 1384) of A. Diabelli et Comp. Although this is, unfortunately, not the original edition, as is shown by the publishers' mark "C. et D. No. 1384" inside [Cappi und Diabelli changed their firm-name to "A. Diabelli und Comp." in 1824; the inside mark argues the use of the original plates], it is doubtless a reimpression corrected by Beethoven himself (in 1823, acc. to Nottebohm: "Beethoveniana," 1872, p. 6). For the above-mentioned double trill it has the following fingering:

In view of the arbitrary manner in which Diabelli treated op. 120, later, the possibility is certainly not wholly excluded, that alterations were

* "'The following sonatas [op. 110 and 111] were engraved in Paris, in order to make a very brilliant appearance; one was corrected by Mr. Moscheles,' writes Schlesinger, on July 2, 1822." (Nohl: "Beethoven's Leben," III, p. 878.) [Probably op. 110; *cf.* what follows above.]

† *Sonate / pour le Piano Forte / Composée & très respectuesement* [sic] *Dediée / à Son Altesse Impériale Monseigneur / l'Archiduc Rodolphe d'Autriche / Cardinal Prince Archévêque d'Olmütz &c. &c. / Par / Louis de Beethoven* [To the left] *Œuv. 111 . . .* [To the right] *Prix* [omitted] *Propriété des Editeurs. / Paris, / chez / Maurice Schlesinger Editeur, Rue de Richelieu No. 107 /* [To the left] *Berlin, chez A. M. Schlesinger, / Editeur Libraire et Md de Musique.* [To the right] *Vienne, chez S. A. Steiner et Cie Artaria et Cie Sauer et Leidersdorff.* [sic] *Londres, chez Boosey et Cie Chappel et Cie et Muzio Clementi et Compie.*—Doubtless the original edition. The publishing house of Sauer & Leidesdorf, mentioned in the title, had existed since about 1823, and continued (acc. to Schilling) only till about 1828.

made here in the later editions; the figures 5 4, too, are somewhat larger than 1 2, and the periods are lacking.—But in the Royal Library there is an old edition of this same sonata by A. M. Schlesinger (Berlin), which follows, in the upper part of its title-page as far as the word "Beethoven," even in typography, the title of the above-mentioned Paris edition,* though the inner engraving is different. This edition also gives the fingering for the double trill:

It was a piece of good fortune that we examined this edition in the Royal Library; for we had already found another copy with just the same title. The courteous reader, to whom our circumstantiality in quotation may have long been a matter for surprise, will be duly grateful for our caution. In this later edition, which we could readily recognize as such by the excision of a short variant, and for other reasons, some proof-reader reversed the figures, making 4. 5. out of 5. 4.—Finally we will mention, that Breitkopf & Härtel's Complete Edition likewise gives the fingering {54/12; while the Czerny-Simrock edition has no fingering whatever in this passage.

The third and last case has to do with the Bagatellen, op. 119 (or, as given in earlier editions, op. 112). The passage in question is in the 7th Bagatelle in C major, three-four time, measures 1 and 2:

* It may have used the old title-page. "Dediée" is corrected to "Dédiée."—It continues: Op. 111 . . . . Pr. 1½Thlr. / Propriété des Editeurs. / Berlin chez A^d. M^t. Schlesinger, Editeur Libraire et M^d. de Musique. / [To the left] Paris, M. Schlesinger. . . . [To the right] Londres, Boosey & Cie / Einzig rechtmässige Originalausgabe. / S. 1160.

96

which are fingered in several of the earliest editions. Our attention was
called by the publishers to an edition by Sauer & Leidesdorf (No. 700),
which (as op. 112) was composed, according to Nottebohm, in 1824. In
it our two measures appear as follows, in the upper staff:

Certain imperfections on this page, such as the evidently later inser-
tion, as a correction, of the tempo-mark " Allegro ma non troppo," also
the omitted *tr* in meas. 1, the strange " 45 ou 34," etc., made this passage appear doubtful. And, in fact, the tempo-mark is wanting in a
copy in the Royal Library, though the fingering, to be sure, is the same.
The copy in the Royal Library therefore represents an earlier edition.
The business was soon taken over by Diabelli & Co.,* who retained the
old plates with the register D. et C., No. 2224; consequently these two
measures give (the edition is, we believe, still in print) an exact coun-
terpart of the edition by Sauer & Leidesdorf first described. As these
eleven Bagatelles were first published (acc. to Nottebohm) at Paris in
1823, by Schlesinger, we also made a search for this edition, but are able
to quote only from Brandus et C[ie], whose edition, according to the publisher's mark " M.S. 129," and the high page-numbers, is part of the
Paris Schlesinger's Complete Edition. Here the fingering and tempo-
mark agree with the later edition of Sauer & Leidesdorf. But, as we
were unable to regard these editions as containing the original markings,
and as Breitkopf & Härtel's Complete Edition (based, according to the
prospectus, on a wealth of original sources) gives neither the tempo-
mark nor the fingering in question, we felt obliged to continue our search.
Nottebohm states that Starke's Pianoforte-Method contains, in its third
volume (1821), the earliest impression of the particular Bagatelle and
four others; this volume was lacking in the Royal Library. Finally,
however, through the kindness of its custos, Dr. Kopfermann, and the

* *Cf.* Nottebohm, " Them. Verzeichniss," and our Note on p. 84.

friendly aid of Messrs. G. Nottebohm and C. F. Pohl, in Vienna, we were enabled to obtain this volume, though only in the second edition. But we are assured by Mr. Pohl, the archivist of the " Gesellschaft der Musikfreunde " in Vienna, that it precisely agrees with the first in the matters in question.

On p. 71, at the very beginning, the " trifle " referred to :

Now, although it is not stated (as in the second volume of the Method, at Beethoven's op. 28, movements II and III) that the fingering was marked by Beethoven himself, we think it most likely that such is the case (in this fifth Bagatelle the fingering is marked in only one other place) ; it would seem, therefore, that we have found one definite case in which Beethoven began the trill on the principal note.*

We abstain from building up extended hypotheses upon this fact, which we discovered only at the close of our investigation. Yet we cannot avoid seeing, that this case might justify the most far-reaching conclusions, so that even the third of our above hypotheses—according to which Beethoven began only those trills on the auxiliary when such a beginning is explicitly required by an appoggiatura or the fingerings with which we are now acquainted—gains a high degree of probability.†

Before going to this extreme, however, it should be established (1) that the last-mentioned fingerings for the 7th Bagatelle, op. 119, do not

* There must exist an original English edition of these Bagatelles, which would either confirm this opinion, or (which can hardly be assumed now) contradict it. [*Cf.* Nohl, " Neue Briefe Beethoven's " letter to Ries of Feb., 1823, and July 16, 1823.]

† We should then have to assume, for Beethoven's explanations of the trill in op. 53, that the composer had expected the indicated execution even without writing the appoggiatura ; or else that the appoggiatura had been forgotten here. According to the editions of J. Riedl, Czerny-Simrock, and Breitkopf & Härtel, this trill-*g*, moreover, is tied over from the preceding measure ; and it therefore remains doubtful whether Beethoven did not, eight measures further back, begin the measure with the auxiliary (or when, if not then ?).

form an exception (for which we are unable to bring forward any
cogent reason), and (2) that Carl Czerny either had no idea whatever
of his master's style of trill-playing [!],* or simply followed his own
views (or conjectures) in opposition to his better knowledge, in the
directions for the trill which we have quoted, and which were written
down during the composer's lifetime, and even almost under his eyes.
We can find no answer to these two questions for our readers. On the
other hand, we will observe, that Beethoven in all probability began

not only the next trills in this Bagatelle , on the

principal note, but possibly also the long closing trill in the bass

 etc. This latter assumption is fortified by

the circumstance, that the after-beat of the trill is indicated by a 32d-

note :  For if we take into consideration, that

in the given tempo, "Allegro ma non troppo," the rapidity of the trill
could hardly be otherwise expressed than by 32d-notes, this after-beat
(supposing the trill to have begun on the principal note) fits admirably
into the general movement :

* Yet Beethoven, in his later years, went through several important compositions with Czerny, and attended their performance ! (About 1818 ? *Cf.* Schindler,
Biography, 1st ed., p. 110.) These are evidently the same Beethoven matinées
which took place [Schindler, 3d ed.] every Sunday from 10 to 11 in the win-
ters of 1818–20 at Czerny's rooms, in which other artists also took part, and which
Beethoven frequently attended in 1818. But, judging from this passage, Beethoven does not appear to have been specially edified by Czerny's productions.
Schindler affects to have learned much from his " critical remarks," etc.

We will observe, finally, that the style of trill which we proposed in the general part of this Preface, which is often adopted by Czerny, and begins on the principal note, *e.g.,*

etc.,

or, as J. B. Cramer would write:

etc.,

appears to be excluded both by the peculiar notation:

and by the requirement that the trill should begin the next measure on the principal note:

The patient reader, who has followed us to this point, will regard it as a matter of course that we, in our concert-editions, have always indicated by our fingerings at *tr* the execution which seemed most in keeping with the results of our historical investigations. He will also comprehend, that we could not well put off the publication of our instructive concert-editions until the question of the trill should be finally settled; the question itself being, through our latest investigation (which owes its inception to a mere accident), carried on to a new stage, and still further away from final solution. Lastly, we trust that he will be grateful to us for choosing the way of historical investigation for the solution of this question, which has long been a burning one, instead of offering our subjective opinion. We have arrived at some positive conclusions, and therefore (and in part for our own justification) considered that we ought not to withhold from our readers the results of several years' study; we hope, too, that others who feel drawn to studies of this kind, will continue the investigation in various directions from the foundation already laid. Meanwhile subjective opinion, which begins where historical information ends, may also maintain its rights.

In closing, we beg to thank the gentlemen who have aided us in our arduous labors; first of all the custos of the Royal Library, Herr Dr. Albert Kopfermann, who not only most amiably facilitated the editor's very frequent utilization of the Library, but, by sacrificing his own time, made it possible to procure much important material. We likewise owe sincere thanks to Herr Ober-Kapellmeister Wilhelm Taubert for procuring very valuable original editions. And to all the gentlemen who favored the editor with information of any kind, he begs to assure his lasting gratitude.

A CATALOG OF SELECTED
DOVER BOOKS
IN ALL FIELDS OF INTEREST

A CATALOG OF SELECTED DOVER
BOOKS IN ALL FIELDS OF INTEREST

100 BEST-LOVED POEMS, Edited by Philip Smith. "The Passionate Shepherd to His Love," "Shall I compare thee to a summer's day?" "Death, be not proud," "The Raven," "The Road Not Taken," plus works by Blake, Wordsworth, Byron, Shelley, Keats, many others. 96pp. 5³⁄₁₆ x 8¼. 0-486-28553-7

100 SMALL HOUSES OF THE THIRTIES, Brown-Blodgett Company. Exterior photographs and floor plans for 100 charming structures. Illustrations of models accompanied by descriptions of interiors, color schemes, closet space, and other amenities. 200 illustrations. 112pp. 8⅜ x 11. 0-486-44131-8

1000 TURN-OF-THE-CENTURY HOUSES: With Illustrations and Floor Plans, Herbert C. Chivers. Reproduced from a rare edition, this showcase of homes ranges from cottages and bungalows to sprawling mansions. Each house is meticulously illustrated and accompanied by complete floor plans. 256pp. 9⅜ x 12¼.
0-486-45596-3

101 GREAT AMERICAN POEMS, Edited by The American Poetry & Literacy Project. Rich treasury of verse from the 19th and 20th centuries includes works by Edgar Allan Poe, Robert Frost, Walt Whitman, Langston Hughes, Emily Dickinson, T. S. Eliot, other notables. 96pp. 5³⁄₁₆ x 8¼. 0-486-40158-8

101 GREAT SAMURAI PRINTS, Utagawa Kuniyoshi. Kuniyoshi was a master of the warrior woodblock print — and these 18th-century illustrations represent the pinnacle of his craft. Full-color portraits of renowned Japanese samurais pulse with movement, passion, and remarkably fine detail. 112pp. 8⅜ x 11. 0-486-46523-3

ABC OF BALLET, Janet Grosser. Clearly worded, abundantly illustrated little guide defines basic ballet-related terms: arabesque, battement, pas de chat, relevé, sissonne, many others. Pronunciation guide included. Excellent primer. 48pp. 4³⁄₁₆ x 5¾.
0-486-40871-X

ACCESSORIES OF DRESS: An Illustrated Encyclopedia, Katherine Lester and Bess Viola Oerke. Illustrations of hats, veils, wigs, cravats, shawls, shoes, gloves, and other accessories enhance an engaging commentary that reveals the humor and charm of the many-sided story of accessorized apparel. 644 figures and 59 plates. 608pp. 6 ⅛ x 9¼.
0-486-43378-1

ADVENTURES OF HUCKLEBERRY FINN, Mark Twain. Join Huck and Jim as their boyhood adventures along the Mississippi River lead them into a world of excitement, danger, and self-discovery. Humorous narrative, lyrical descriptions of the Mississippi valley, and memorable characters. 224pp. 5³⁄₁₆ x 8¼. 0-486-28061-6

ALICE STARMORE'S BOOK OF FAIR ISLE KNITTING, Alice Starmore. A noted designer from the region of Scotland's Fair Isle explores the history and techniques of this distinctive, stranded-color knitting style and provides copious illustrated instructions for 14 original knitwear designs. 208pp. 8⅜ x 10⅞. 0-486-47218-9

Browse over 9,000 books at www.doverpublications.com

ALICE'S ADVENTURES IN WONDERLAND, Lewis Carroll. Beloved classic about a little girl lost in a topsy-turvy land and her encounters with the White Rabbit, March Hare, Mad Hatter, Cheshire Cat, and other delightfully improbable characters. 42 illustrations by Sir John Tenniel. 96pp. 5⁵⁄₁₆ x 8¼.   0-486-27543-4

AMERICA'S LIGHTHOUSES: An Illustrated History, Francis Ross Holland. Profusely illustrated fact-filled survey of American lighthouses since 1716. Over 200 stations — East, Gulf, and West coasts, Great Lakes, Hawaii, Alaska, Puerto Rico, the Virgin Islands, and the Mississippi and St. Lawrence Rivers. 240pp. 8 x 10¾.
0-486-25576-X

AN ENCYCLOPEDIA OF THE VIOLIN, Alberto Bachmann. Translated by Frederick H. Martens. Introduction by Eugene Ysaye. First published in 1925, this renowned reference remains unsurpassed as a source of essential information, from construction and evolution to repertoire and technique. Includes a glossary and 73 illustrations. 496pp. 6⅛ x 9¼.   0-486-46618-3

ANIMALS: 1,419 Copyright-Free Illustrations of Mammals, Birds, Fish, Insects, etc., Selected by Jim Harter. Selected for its visual impact and ease of use, this outstanding collection of wood engravings presents over 1,000 species of animals in extremely lifelike poses. Includes mammals, birds, reptiles, amphibians, fish, insects, and other invertebrates. 284pp. 9 x 12.   0-486-23766-4

THE ANNALS, Tacitus. Translated by Alfred John Church and William Jackson Brodribb. This vital chronicle of Imperial Rome, written by the era's great historian, spans A.D. 14-68 and paints incisive psychological portraits of major figures, from Tiberius to Nero. 416pp. 5⁵⁄₁₆ x 8¼.   0-486-45236-0

ANTIGONE, Sophocles. Filled with passionate speeches and sensitive probing of moral and philosophical issues, this powerful and often-performed Greek drama reveals the grim fate that befalls the children of Oedipus. Footnotes. 64pp. 5⁵⁄₁₆ x 8 ¼.   0-486-27804-2

ART DECO DECORATIVE PATTERNS IN FULL COLOR, Christian Stoll. Reprinted from a rare 1910 portfolio, 160 sensuous and exotic images depict a breathtaking array of florals, geometrics, and abstracts — all elegant in their stark simplicity. 64pp. 8⅜ x 11.   0-486-44862-2

THE ARTHUR RACKHAM TREASURY: 86 Full-Color Illustrations, Arthur Rackham. Selected and Edited by Jeff A. Menges. A stunning treasury of 86 full-page plates span the famed English artist's career, from *Rip Van Winkle* (1905) to masterworks such as *Undine, A Midsummer Night's Dream,* and *Wind in the Willows* (1939). 96pp. 8⅜ x 11.
0-486-44685-9

THE AUTHENTIC GILBERT & SULLIVAN SONGBOOK, W. S. Gilbert and A. S. Sullivan. The most comprehensive collection available, this songbook includes selections from every one of Gilbert and Sullivan's light operas. Ninety-two numbers are presented uncut and unedited, and in their original keys. 410pp. 9 x 12.
0-486-23482-7

THE AWAKENING, Kate Chopin. First published in 1899, this controversial novel of a New Orleans wife's search for love outside a stifling marriage shocked readers. Today, it remains a first-rate narrative with superb characterization. New introductory Note. 128pp. 5⁵⁄₁₆ x 8¼.   0-486-27786-0

BASIC DRAWING, Louis Priscilla. Beginning with perspective, this commonsense manual progresses to the figure in movement, light and shade, anatomy, drapery, composition, trees and landscape, and outdoor sketching. Black-and-white illustrations throughout. 128pp. 8⅜ x 11.   0-486-45815-6

THE BATTLES THAT CHANGED HISTORY, Fletcher Pratt. Historian profiles 16 crucial conflicts, ancient to modern, that changed the course of Western civilization. Gripping accounts of battles led by Alexander the Great, Joan of Arc, Ulysses S. Grant, other commanders. 27 maps. 352pp. 5⅜ x 8½.   0-486-41129-X

BEETHOVEN'S LETTERS, Ludwig van Beethoven. Edited by Dr. A. C. Kalischer. Features 457 letters to fellow musicians, friends, greats, patrons, and literary men. Reveals musical thoughts, quirks of personality, insights, and daily events. Includes 15 plates. 410pp. 5⅜ x 8½.   0-486-22769-3

BERNICE BOBS HER HAIR AND OTHER STORIES, F. Scott Fitzgerald. This brilliant anthology includes 6 of Fitzgerald's most popular stories: "The Diamond as Big as the Ritz," the title tale, "The Offshore Pirate," "The Ice Palace," "The Jelly Bean," and "May Day." 176pp. 5⅜ x 8½.   0-486-47049-0

BESLER'S BOOK OF FLOWERS AND PLANTS: 73 Full-Color Plates from Hortus Eystettensis, 1613, Basilius Besler. Here is a selection of magnificent plates from the *Hortus Eystettensis,* which vividly illustrated and identified the plants, flowers, and trees that thrived in the legendary German garden at Eichstätt. 80pp. 8⅜ x 11.
0-486-46005-3

THE BOOK OF KELLS, Edited by Blanche Cirker. Painstakingly reproduced from a rare facsimile edition, this volume contains full-page decorations, portraits, illustrations, plus a sampling of textual leaves with exquisite calligraphy and ornamentation. 32 full-color illustrations. 32pp. 9⅜ x 12¼.   0-486-24345-1

THE BOOK OF THE CROSSBOW: With an Additional Section on Catapults and Other Siege Engines, Ralph Payne-Gallwey. Fascinating study traces history and use of crossbow as military and sporting weapon, from Middle Ages to modern times. Also covers related weapons: balistas, catapults, Turkish bows, more. Over 240 illustrations. 400pp. 7¼ x 10⅛.   0-486-28720-3

THE BUNGALOW BOOK: Floor Plans and Photos of 112 Houses, 1910, Henry L. Wilson. Here are 112 of the most popular and economic blueprints of the early 20th century — plus an illustration or photograph of each completed house. A wonderful time capsule that still offers a wealth of valuable insights. 160pp. 8⅜ x 11.
0-486-45104-6

THE CALL OF THE WILD, Jack London. A classic novel of adventure, drawn from London's own experiences as a Klondike adventurer, relating the story of a heroic dog caught in the brutal life of the Alaska Gold Rush. Note. 64pp. 5³⁄₁₆ x 8¼.
0-486-26472-6

CANDIDE, Voltaire. Edited by Francois-Marie Arouet. One of the world's great satires since its first publication in 1759. Witty, caustic skewering of romance, science, philosophy, religion, government — nearly all human ideals and institutions. 112pp. 5³⁄₁₆ x 8¼.   0-486-26689-3

CELEBRATED IN THEIR TIME: Photographic Portraits from the George Grantham Bain Collection, Edited by Amy Pastan. With an Introduction by Michael Carlebach. Remarkable portrait gallery features 112 rare images of Albert Einstein, Charlie Chaplin, the Wright Brothers, Henry Ford, and other luminaries from the worlds of politics, art, entertainment, and industry. 128pp. 8⅜ x 11.   0-486-46754-6

CHARIOTS FOR APOLLO: The NASA History of Manned Lunar Spacecraft to 1969, Courtney G. Brooks, James M. Grimwood, and Loyd S. Swenson, Jr. This illustrated history by a trio of experts is the definitive reference on the Apollo spacecraft and lunar modules. It traces the vehicles' design, development, and operation in space. More than 100 photographs and illustrations. 576pp. 6¾ x 9¼. 0-486-46756-2